TAKE THE LAW INTO YOUR OWN HANDS™

Victims' Rights

A Complete Guide to Crime Victim Compensation

D1450747

William L. Ginsburg
Attorney at Law

SPHINX PUBLISHING
Sphinx International, Inc.
1725 Clearwater-Largo Rd. S.
Post Office Box 25
Clearwater, FL 34617
(813) 587-0999

Note: The law changes constantly and is subject to different interpretations. It is up to you to check it thoroughly before relying on it. Neither the author nor the publisher guarantees the outcome of the uses to which this material may be put.

First Edition, 1994

Library of Congress Number: 94-65393
ISBN 0-913825-82-4

Manufactured in the United States of America.

This publication is designed to provide accurate and authoritative information in regard to the subject matter covered. It is sold with the understanding that the publisher is not engaged in rendering legal, accounting or other professional services. If legal advice or other expert assistance is required, the service of a competent professional person should be sought.

-From a Declaration of Principles jointly adopted by a Committee of the American Bar Association and a Committee of Publishers.

Published by Sphinx Publishing, a division of Sphinx International, Inc., Post Office Box 25, Clearwater, Florida 34617-0025. This publication is available through most book stores but if you cannot find it locally you can order it by mail for $12.95 plus $3.00 shipping. Florida residents please add sales tax. For credit card orders call 1-800-226-5291.

Table of Contents

Introduction

Life in these United States now includes the high probability that you or someone you know will become the victim of a violent crime. The slaying of James Jordan, father and best friend of basketball star Michael Jordan, reminds us that anyone can become the victim of a mindless, random, violent crime. Today, all fifty of our states, as well as the District of Columbia and the Virgin Islands, have established agencies which compensate victims of violent crimes. These are federally-supported agencies which have as their sole purpose the reimbursement of victims of violent crime and, in certain instances, their dependents and others. The existence of these readily available sources of compensation could be America's best kept secret. Relatively speaking, few victims ever find relief.

Now that has all changed. This is, in part, due to the emergence of this book which includes a complete listing of agencies, offices, and telephone numbers of those who compensate victims. Until now, the responsibility for victim awareness of the existence of these funds rested mainly on the police and prosecutors.

When I was a small child, I loved to listen to a radio program called, "Mr. District Attorney." It began with the following statement. (I may be slightly misquoting the announcer, but this is close enough to make the point.) "It shall be the duty of the District Attorney, not only to prosecute all crimes committed within his jurisdiction but to defend with equal vigor, the rights and privileges of all its citizens." When that speech was first uttered, it was romantic fiction. Now it is reality. It is the duty of the District Attorney (or Prosecutor, Prosecuting Attorney, or State Attorney, depending upon what title is used in your state) to advise you as to your rights and to inform you as to any agency which has been created to come to your aid. Despite this, estimates indicate that as low as ten per cent of all victims ever recover anything from these funds.

This book can make you aware of what you need to know in language you can readily understand. It is my avowed intention to increase the awareness of violent crime victims as to their right to compensation through publication and distribution of this book.

Chapter 1
In The Beginning

The violent crime victims relief fund began as a federal concept which, in turn, became a series of funds administered by the individual states who have adapted their own rules which vary widely from state to state.

I first became aware of the existence of these funds as a result of a case which occurred in Indiana. I thought I was representing the parents of a child who died as the result of a violent crime. It turned out they were not actually the biological parents of the victim. They were, however, his legal guardians. Under Indiana rules, the fact that they were legal guardians, but not biological parents did not matter. They were eligible for reimbursement for all funeral-related expenses. In addition, Indiana rules permit the hiring of a private attorney in order to assist the claimant in the preparation and processing of their claim. The rules further provide for reimbursement of that cost, limited by what the state terms, "a reasonable amount." In Indiana, that can be up to $1,250, depending on the complexity of the claim.

Often, the rules provide that certain items included as part of the claim, such as funeral expenses, have a maximum amount, known as a "cap." In addition, in most states there is absolutely no allowance for pain or suffering. These laws are strictly interpreted as reimbursement for financial loss. Finally, there is always a limited amount of time allowed for you to complete your claim.

It is in your best interest to learn about the elements that make up your claim in general, and when you feel you understand them, you can turn to the section of this book which contains the rules which apply in your situation.

Chapter 2
What Is Violence?

The first event you must prove is that a crime actually occurred and that it was violent. In determining whether violence is present in your case, consider the following discussion.

You can begin with this question. Was a weapon used in the commission of the crime which victimized you? The answer is clear if there was a weapon present. That is, by definition, a violent crime. But what if the victim truly believed there was a weapon, but the facts later determine there was not. If the victim's belief was based upon the acts of the criminal and that belief was reasonable under the circumstances, the test of violence is met. The key is what is reasonable.

If the victim believed a toy gun in the hand of the perpetrator was real, that is sufficient. No one requires you to be shot in order to prove your fear was accurate.

9

Fear can also exist without the presence of a weapon. For example, an older couple may be terrorized by a gang of youthful thugs. Their fists are their weapons. The potential for bodily harm is sufficient to satisfy the statute. Potential violence is violence.

If physical force is directed against you in the course of the crime, whether or not you are actually struck is of no significance. As we lawyers say, "if you were not battered, you still were assaulted." Assault is the reasonable fear of being struck or harmed, which meets the definition of violence.

There is a situation quite similar to the case where the victim believes a weapon is present. This occurs when the victim believes the criminal to be intoxicated. Apparent intoxication on the part of the criminal could be sufficient reason for the victim to believe violence would likely occur. This policy is based solely on the intoxicated appearance of the criminal. You have more to fear from a criminal who seems out of control due to inebriation. Available statistics seem to back up this contention.

Testing the criminal for blood alcohol content after the crime has occurred may confirm the reasonableness of the victim's fear. A subsequent confession by the criminal may also serve to confirm the victim's contention that the defendant was apparently out of control. Where the substance involved is a drug rather than alcohol, the result is the same.

You have the right to request that the criminal be drug tested where you believe such a test would be appropriate. Most law enforcement agents will readily agree to your request based upon your description of the apparent criminal behavior.

Behavior is the key to this discussion. A good example is the relatively new crime called "stalking." This crime occurs when the victim is intensively pursued by the criminal. Celebrities, wealthy individuals, former partners in personal relationships as well as single custodial parents are typical potential victims. The victim is often terrorized by the details of the chase. The potential for violence contained within this situation is real.

Another example of behavior which could be interpreted by the victim as violent exists where the victim is captured and held against his will. Actual violence may not happen but, once again, the test is the reasonableness of the fear which is likely to occur in the mind of the victim.

There are basically four situations where you don't have to prove violence ever existed, but you do have to establish that certain other conditions did exist. These are:

1. Where the victim was injured in a traffic accident in which the wrongdoer was either partially or totally under the influence of alcohol or drugs. In this instance, you may not even be aware that the other driver is intoxicated. That doesn't matter. If there is a crash and the other driver had alcohol in his or her system, that is sufficient. The same is true where there is no crash but the other driver commits a crime while under the influence of alcohol.

2. Where a crime involves a sexual assault. Again, it is not necessary to prove that violence actually occurred.

11

Here the test is not violence but that the act which occurred is a sexual assault prohibited by law. You can also assert that the victim, or a close family member of the victim, would benefit from counseling. If you can establish the need for counseling, which usually is the case, you have met the requirement of the Victims of Violent Crimes Act. Again you are cautioned: This varies from state to state, but at least you are now aware that the possibility of compensation exists.

3. Where the victim was attempting to assist a law enforcement officer in the course of his duty. This could happen, for example, where you observe an officer involved in a high speed chase, and you attempt to either pursue the criminal or assist in termination of the criminal flight.

4. Where the victim attempts to prevent a crime from occurring. For example, you are in a convenience store and you believe that another person in the store is carrying a weapon and you attempt to prevent the robbery you are certain will occur. It turns out that you were right about the robbery but wrong about the weapon. You mistake about the weapon does not matter, you are still within the intent of the law. You were trying to stop a crime from taking place.

What is the rationale behind these four exceptions to the general rule which requires you to prove violence occurred? Two possibilities present themselves for consideration: First, some situations are so packed with the potential for violence that public policy requires inclusion in the Victims of Violent Crimes Act. Second, we recognize that certain individuals will perform heroic deeds and the potential for bodily harm on those occasions is enormous. The authors of the act wanted to be sure that no good deed goes uncompensated.

Chapter 3
What Is A Crime?

The test to determine your eligibility for compensation is not the definition of what is a crime, but, rather, which crimes are included by your state as appropriate for compensation. Again, this will vary on a state by state basis.

In general, crimes are classified by either the severity of the prohibited behavior or the severity of the applicable punishment. The more severe offenses are called felonies and the less severe are categorized as misdemeanors. Misdemeanors and felonies are often further grouped by degree of severity. A typical test is as follows: Crimes punishable by jail sentences in excess of one year are usually felonies. Crimes punishable by jail sentences of one year or less are usually treated as misdemeanors.

There is an important difference as far as the victim is concerned. As a general rule, all felonies are considered compensable as far as the term "crime" is concerned but not

15

all misdemeanors are included on the list of potentially compensable crimes. Remember, drunk driving offenses can also be included as compensable even when the basic charge is just a misdemeanor.

Drunk driving is usually the single exception to the felony rule, although a thorough review of all of the state rules and regulations may produce other exceptions.

Chapter 4
Eligibility Requirements

Normally, you must file your claim in the state where the crime took place. More often than not, that is the state where you live. But what happens when the crime took place elsewhere, away from the state where you reside? The law directs you to file in the state where the crime took place. Other than the added difficulty of processing your claim from a distant place, usually there is no other difference. The law of that state controls, even if the benefits are lower than they would be in your own state.

But what happens when a non-resident is barred from collection, or where the rules of your state and the state where the crime occurred are grossly inconsistent? In those circumstances, some states permit you to file in your native state. Conventional wisdom (common sense) tells you to check the rules in both jurisdictions and follow the rules. First, check the law where the crime took place. If you encounter difficulty, check with your local state prosecutor. If you are still not satisfied, ask the prosecutor to direct you to the appropriate violent crime commission.

The crime must have been reported to the police as quickly as possible. Most states require this to done within either 24 or 48 hours immediately following the crime. In addition, the claimant or the victim must cooperate with the police authorities.

There does not have to be a conviction resulting from the prosecution of the crime. This is not a necessary element of the victim's claim for compensation. Sometimes, the alleged culprit is never apprehended, nor is his true identity ever known.

The prosecution of a major crime is often a lengthy and time consuming event. The prosecution can and often does, take longer than the time allocated to the victim for the completion of his or her claim. The fact that prosecution has commenced but has not finished, does not invalidate the claim. The claim remains valid even if the defendant is eventually found not guilty. Guilt or innocence has nothing to do with the determination that a violent crime did, in fact, take place.

In one other vital respect, time is very important. In all jurisdictions, you have a very limited amount of time to file and complete your claim for compensation. Most jurisdictions allow you one or two years from the date of the crime to complete your claim. Since it is almost a certainty that some part of what you submit will be rejected or returned to you for correction and that takes time to correct, do not wait until the last possible moment to initially submit your claim. In addition, time is also necessary for the Commission to consider your claim, and you definitely do not want a hurried decision.

Typically, the Commission requires that you claim expenses of $100.00 or more. The reasoning behind this requirement is two-fold. First, the cost to the state of processing your claim is such that it is economically unfeasible for the state to process minor claims. Simply put, it costs too much and the cost of processing has to be taken from the funds available.

Second, the fund was created to offset catastrophic losses which the average family or individual cannot bear. Medical expenses, for example, can be horrendous. It is important that you know this requirement exists and that you comply with the requirement as part of your initial application.

Chapter 5
Who Can Qualify?

Not only victims qualify for these benefits. Certain others can also obtain compensation.

In order to understand who qualifies besides victims, it is necessary to first establish who is or is not a victim. All "others" must bear a relationship of one kind or another to the victim. A victim is someone who suffers death or bodily injury (or in some states, property damage) as a direct result of the commission of a violent crime.

Where death has occurred, and the victim was married, the surviving spouse is eligible for relief. The survivor must pay for medical expenses incurred, as well as funeral and burial costs. This is not meant to be a complete list of what expenses may be recovered, but only to show you why the survivor is eligible. A complete list of expenses for which recovery is possible, will follow in a latter chapter of this book.

21

It is also possible that the spouse can recover where death has not occurred. Expenses then become the burden of the victim and not necessarily of the survivor. The survivor may suffer different losses. Each case is different and help is readily available to enable the parties involved to sort out who should be filing the claim. You can call the prosecutor and ask for Victims Assistance. They should be able to answer your questions.

Where death has occurred or where the victim survived but cannot work, dependents have a right to recovery. These are usually the children of the victim. There also may be other so called, "legal dependents" who qualify. If you feel that you or someone you represent falls into that category, but you are not certain, ask your prosecutor.

In addition, parents or legal guardians who have paid out sums of money in excess of $100.00 on behalf of their victimized child or legal ward are also eligible for reimbursement. Documentation such as a birth certificate, adoption papers, or letters of legal guardianship, will be required. These papers should be obtained immediately, and submitted along with your application.

Third-party service providers are also eligible for payment under the act. Generally speaking, these are either health care professionals or attorneys who assist in claim preparation and processing and any other entities who provide appropriate services such as a funeral service or burial.

The typical third-party provider is subject to caps or limitations to the amount they can collect. Most states specify what they can charge. For example, most states provide up to $3,000.00 for funeral expenses.

Every claimant under this act must complete an application form in order to apply for compensation. This application form advises the claimant that third party providers may be paid directly by the fund. The claimant is further advised that by applying for compensation, the claimant expressly authorizes the fund to pay such providers directly.

Attorneys are allowed to assist claimants in processing their claim for what is referred to as, "a reasonable fee." The state considers ten to fifteen per cent of the total amount of compensation to be reasonable. Many states provide arbitration in the event of a dispute over the amount of the attorney fee awarded to the claimant, or in direct payment to the attorney.

The final category of third-party providers are those described in the various acts as, "entities." While the word seems ambiguous at best, there is a simple enough explanation. It would be impossible to enumerate all of the possible third party providers. Because a specific class of third party provider is not mentioned in the act does not mean it is excluded from consideration.

An example of this type of "entity" might be a florist who provides flowers at the funeral and then later at the grave site. Where the victim cannot claim direct compensation and therefore does not pay this bill, it is still possible for the florist to be paid directly. Another example might be one who provides counseling for a relative of the victim even though that relative is not a spouse of the victim or a dependent of the victim. Under the act, that relative is not directly eligible for compensation but services rendered to that person might be brought in under the entity provision.

Twenty-five percent of the states still apply a means test. That means if you either make too much money, or simply have too much money, you can be declared ineligible regardless of all other circumstances. Eight states have a deductible feature similar to what you will find in some automobile policies. Check the list you will find in the latter part of this book to see what your state has decided regarding a means test.

Chapter 6
Disqualifications

According to an information pamphlet issued by one state's Violent Crime Compensation Division, there are four situations where otherwise qualified individuals may be precluded from compensation.

Remember, no matter how cut and dried the rulings may appear to be, there are always exceptions to every rule. You have the right to discuss your particular situation with the Commission. If you are not satisfied with the answer you receive, you have the option of further discussing your problem with the attorney who is retained by the Commission. If all else fails, you have the right to hire your own attorney to pursue your claim.

First, if you are a victim of a violent crime but did not sustain a bodily injury, you may not recover any sum of money from the fund. However, recent changes in the law in some states permit up to $500.00 in recovery for property damage caused by the crime. If this applies to you, contact the Violent Crime Compensation Commission in your state. Rules usually create their own exceptions.

Second, prisoners, while confined in a correctional institution, are not eligible for compensation through the fund even though they do sustain bodily injury or death. The federal government, when creating guidelines, did not mandate each and every one of the rules and their exceptions. The states put in this and other conditions they believed to be appropriate. The states, in their wisdom, felt this was not the group of people they wanted to benefit.

Third, if you were the victim of an automobile accident which did not involve either drugs or alcohol, you are not eligible for compensation from the victims fund. Is there an exception to this rule? Possibly. If you were injured as a result of the above mentioned accident and there was a crime involved, there still could be coverage under the fund. Not every crime qualifies as an exception to the rule. If the accident occurred because the other party was fleeing the scene of a crime he committed, that would probably be sufficient but where the crime was an expired license, that would not be sufficient because that crime did not contribute to the accident.

Fourth, a victim who, by his own action, contributed to the crime or caused the crime that led to his death or bodily injury is not eligible. This is based upon a combination of two different principles of law which we have brought forward from the old English "Common Law" and made part of our current legal system:

1. No one may benefit from their own criminal act.
2. No one may benefit where they substantially contributed to the wrongful act of another.

Even under these circumstances, there is still room to argue. While you may choose to admit that you contributed to the crime, you can still argue that your contribution to the crime had nothing to do with the cause of the injury sustained. In effect, there is no causal relationship between the crime and the injury. You can also argue that your contribution was minimal, and most importantly, unintentional.

Consider the case of a woman who knew drugs were present in her house, but she never used them or sold them. Her house was burglarized by someone who knew that drugs were in the house. The burglar was armed and she was home alone.

She was awakened by the noise of someone banging around in the living room. She surprised the burglar but it was to no avail as she was not armed. In the ensuing struggle, she was shot in the stomach and nearly died. As a matter of law, she was an accessory to the crime of drug possession because she knew the drugs were in the house, but she was not an accessory to the crime of burglary even though the burglar was after the drugs. The prosecutor insisted that the crimes were intertwined. Perhaps he is right, but this is one instance where I suggested the hiring of a private attorney because there is room for argument. The real message of this case is, once again, rules create their own exceptions.

If you are the victim of a violent crime, you did not contribute to that crime, and you sustained bodily harm or property damage, you are entitled to compensation for your losses. Therefore, you need to know what expenses are covered and what limitations, if any, apply. These matters will be discussed in the following chapter.

Chapter 7
Covered Expenses

For the purpose of this chapter, the "victim" is the person who lost his or her life, or suffered bodily injury or property damage as the result of a violent crime.

The "claimant" is any person claiming financial loss as the direct consequence of the crime. The claimant is not always the same person as the victim. It is possible for the victim to also be the claimant, where he or she does not die or lose legal capacity to pursue the claim on his or her own behalf. If he or she is incapacitated as a result of the crime, a court can appoint a legal guardian on his or her behalf.

Other possible claimants could be a spouse, a dependent, a parent, a legal guardian, a third-party benefit provider, or those loosely categorized as "entities."

The State of Indiana will pay a maximum amount of $10,000.00 to any one claimant whereas my home state of New Mexico, considered by most to be one of the poorest states in the union, will pay $20,000.00 under the same set of circumstances. This is an example of the diversified ways the funds are dispersed. Check the state-by-state listings in this book for the rules which apply in the state where you will be filing your claim.

The list of benefits include medical, surgical, pharmacy, dental, optometry, ambulance services, and outpatient services. Referrals to specialists such as plastic surgeons and physical therapists are also included.

Loss of wages by the victim as a direct result of the crime is also included as compensable under the Act. While there is no cap or limitation to this benefit, you will have to prove your loss by a letter from your employer. You will need a letter from your doctor stating what length of time away from the job is realistic, based upon your injuries.

The underlying presumption in the Act is that the wage earner will be injured. But what if it is the family member who provides child care and is not a wage earner? Such a victim would receive the same medical benefits that the wage earner would receive but this victim, the child care provider, would not be compensated for lost wages. Instead, this child care provider could claim that a substitute child care provider had to be hired, and claim that expense.

In Indiana, for example, up to $1,000.00 can be paid to the victim limited to what was actually paid for child care. Be sure to get receipts as you will have to prove your claim. In addition, the State of Indiana provides up to $500.00 for what they call, "extreme emergencies." Again, check the summary of benefits section of this book for information about your own state.

When it comes to a discussion of loss or damage to your personal property, the picture is best described as confused. Indiana provides two different documents covering loss or damage to personal property. In their information brochure entitled, *Violent Crime Compensation*, they state that, "this fund does not reimburse victims for personal property loss or property damage." The second document is the application for benefits. It contains the same general language, but adds the following paragraph: "Some personal property loss can now be compensable under the program (maximum of $500.00)." A strict legal construction of these two documents read together is that property loss has been added but the situation is not clear as it relates to property damage.

This is an example of an attempt to broaden coverage. The point is that these laws are not carved in stone. These laws, like all laws, are subject to review and change. Coverage of property loss or property damage is far from universal among the states.

Some expenses of the dependents of victims are also subject to compensation.

Indiana, which we are using as our example, will pay up to $3,500.00 for funeral, burial or cremation expenses to whomever paid these expenses. Where surviving dependents need mental health counseling, Indiana will provide up to $1,500.00 to either a mental health facility or a properly licensed counselor.

Surviving dependents can claim loss of financial support but only when the victim died as the result of a violent crime. There is usually no cap or limitation upon this class of claimant other than the maximum amount allowed for the entire claim.

Where the claimant uses the services of an attorney, the amount charged to the claimant can be paid directly to the claimant. That is the result if the claimant has already paid the bill. The state may pay the attorney directly if the bill has not been paid. As already mentioned, this portion of the claim is limited by the rule of reason imposed by the commission.

Chapter 8
"Pain And Suffering"

Other than the controversy over property damage or loss of personal property, there is one major item that is only rarely covered under the Violent Crime Victims Compensation Act. That is what the law calls, "pain and suffering." At the time of publication of this book, pain and suffering compensation is only available through the Act in Hawaii, Rhode Island, Tennessee, West Virginia, and the Virgin Islands. The Act covers monetary losses only in all other states. However, you should ask if any recent changes have been made to your state's law.

In general, the traditional law permits payment for pain and suffering where injuries are involved, but only through a lawsuit. First, you must get a judgment against the wrongdoer. Second, you must collect the judgment, which can be difficult if the wrongdoer does not have any money or other assets. In such a lawsuit there is no government compensation fund available to pay you. Where pain and suffering is a large part of your claim, you may have no alternative but to file a lawsuit.

In every community, there are local attorneys waiting to come to your assistance. Just make sure that your first visit is free. These attorneys often advertise their specialty on television and on outdoor bill boards, as well as in local newspapers.

Expect these attorneys to charge a contingent fee for their services. In English, this means they do not charge a fee unless they win and collect on your behalf. Usually, they work on a percentage basis taking anywhere from one-fourth to one-half of your judgment or settlement.

Occasionally, there may be an insurance company, who represents the defendant, lurking in the background. Although insurance does not usually pay for criminal acts an employer's policy may cover acts committed by employees.

If the act is covered the insuror must pay any judgment or settlement obtained by you or your attorney against their insured. You always have the opportunity to negotiate directly with the insurance company by discussing the matter with their claims representative, However, once you are represented by an attorney, that claims representative can only negotiate with your legal representative.

The decision you make regarding using an attorney is based upon the following: Normally you get a smaller settlement when you do not employ an attorney but you get to keep all that you receive. In my opinion, a competent attorney already is aware of this and considers it his responsibility to get you more net dollars, i.e, dollars you get to keep, as a direct result of his services.

All of this is a proper subject for discussion during your initial free visit with your attorney. Remember, his fees and terms are negotiable and most attorneys will negotiate with you. They want financially lucrative cases and as far as they are concerned, nothing is carved in stone.

If you have difficulty in locating an attorney, contact your state bar association. They will assist you in finding the right attorney for you. This entire subject is covered in detail, in a later chapter of this book.

Chapter 9
What Proof Do You Need?

Always make copies of everything you send to the Violent Crime Compensation Commission in your state or district. Retain those copies in a safe place. Send every thing you mail to the commission, "registered mail, return receipt requested."

First, you must prove that a violent crime took place, and that there was a victim. You must prove that the crime was promptly and properly reported to the police. This is best accomplished by obtaining a copy of the police report and submitting that report as part of the proof of your claim. You can submit this copy attached to your application for compensation.

You must prove that you are either the victim, or one who has a claim, as a direct result of the crime. You do this as part of your application for compensation. If there is no space available as part of the application form, attach a letter addressed to the compensation commission explain-

letter addressed to the compensation commission explaining your particular circumstances and why you are either the victim or the claimant.

Be prepared to prove that you, either as victim or as claimant, fully cooperated with the authorities. Keep a diary showing what day, at what time, and in what manner, you cooperated with the investigators. If this data is requested of you, comply by showing the entries in your diary. Remember, always mail papers "registered mail, return receipt requested." Be prepared to prove that the victim neither contributed to the crime nor benefited from the crime.

These are procedural requirements that are part of each and every claim, but they are just the first part of your claim. In addition, you must prove every expense or cost that is included your claim. You are really talking about two different groups of expenses: the first group consists of those expenses for which you have already paid, and the second group consists of those expenses you have already incurred but have not yet paid.

As to the first group, payment must be made to you, but as to the second group, payment may be made to you or directly to the third-party service provider. The compensation commission will decide the best routing of those payments. Your application form, when empowered by your signature, authorizes the payer to make that decision.

The best possible proof of an expense is the original receipt showing what your payment was for and acknowledging receipt of your money. If you do not have, or never

sion with either your cancelled check, or credit card voucher. If you paid cash, you have no choice but to go back and get another receipt. If some situation makes getting another receipt impossible, write an explanation and include that with your application and other receipts.

Guidelines indicate that, where permitted, reasonable attorneys fees should not exceed 15% of the total sum recovered. If you are employing an attorney to assist you in processing your claim, you should include a letter from your attorney stating and explaining both his services and his fee structure.

Funeral services include coffins, vaults, headstones, graves, preparation of the body, and actual internment or cremation. The receipt must break down these items and show the cost per item. If your receipt shows only one total, you must get the funeral home to give you a second itemized receipt. Send both to the compensation commission after retaining copies for whatever other purposes you may have.

Generally speaking, religious services and direct honorariums to religious personnel are separate. The same rule applies. The receipt must show what services were performed. Other expenses connected with a fatality often include emergency medical transportation from the scene of the crime to an emergency facility. You will be billed for these services and you can recover your costs. Where flowers at the ceremony or internment are considered appropriate, you can submit your receipt for consideration. Where the victim received medical treatment prior to his death, the bill can be submitted for direct payment.

Private health care insurance or public programs like Workers Compensation, Medicaid or Medicare must pay benefits, and the occurrence of a violent crime changes nothing. These payers must pay and their duty to pay is absolute. These violent crime compensation programs have been described as a fund of last resort, and will not pay for something for which other benefits are available.

If the victim survives, and additional services such as physical therapy and counseling are ordered, they are included. Home care may be required and visiting medical personnel often replace the hospital. Their services are also included for compensation.

Family members may also need medical services such as counseling. Here, the key is to show the direct relationship between the need for these services and the crime. The receipt alone is insufficient. You should include a written professional opinion as to the necessity for these services. Remember to also include bills for prescription items, as well as bills for prosthetic devices. These run the gamut from traction devices to artificial limbs. Where the victim needs health care and no private funds are available, advise the medical care facility that the victim is eligible for compensation and they will be paid out of the compensation fund. Conventional wisdom dictates you must stay on top of the situation and make sure everybody follows through and does their job. It will not be quick or easy but you can get it done.

All of the above discussion deals with bills paid, or bills to be paid, but what do you do when you need the fund to pay you money to keep going on with life when the normal bread winner is gone or disabled?

Some compensation plans provide for an emergency payment. This is strictly a one time event with strict limitations. However the key word is "emergency." This is another of those words which require definition. What is an "emergency?" Examples are where there is no money, no food, or household utilities are about to be cut off for non-payment. Essentially, an emergency payment could buy time to hopefully set up a more lasting payment schedule.

Clearly, children of the victim, who cannot create their own income, qualify for payments. However, the fate of a spouse who might be able to get a job is less clear. In this event, the cost of a baby sitter or day care facility may be the only payment authorized. What about elderly parents of the victim, who augmented their meager social security by financial assistance from the victim? Payment in this instance is less likely.

All of these different classifications of dependents have one thing in common: they will have to prove their needs. What constitutes proof as to the amount of their needs? They can start by proving the amount the victim contributed on their behalf. They can also submit a budget which demonstrates whatever amount they need to survive. Finally, the fund administrator has the contacts to obtain any other form of public assistance which may also be available to help the dependents. Both this specific benefit, and the total of all benefits, are limited. Under any set of circumstances, the payments will eventually stop. What you get in the final analysis is time, and time creates the opportunity to create change for the better.

Chapter 10
Time Limitations

Time begins to run against you from the moment the crime is committed. You normally have from one to two years to file your claim depending on the rules of the state where you file your claim. Other parts of the claim procedure have their own individual time limitations which seldom exceed 60 days. Thus you could be timely as far as the entire claim goes, but in trouble because you miss some other time requirement involving only a small part of the claim.

In addition, should you have to appeal part or all of your claim, you will find yourself staring at an additional set of time rules and regulations. With these warning signs indented in your mind, let us review you and your claim from the point of view of time.

For the purpose of this discussion, we will assume the crime took place in Indianapolis, Indiana and that the rules of the State of Indiana govern. That means you have two years from the date of the crime to file your initial application for benefits. That seems fair enough, but here comes the problem. I quote from the bulletin issued by Indiana entitled, *Violent Crime Compensation, Questions and Answers on Financial Assistance to Victims of Violent Crimes:*

> The Violent Crime Compensation Division reviews all applications and investigates to verify the information given and determine the extent of the loss. If the application is not properly completed, or if additional information is required, the Division will send a written explanation to the claimant of what is needed. If a claim is not complete within 30 days of filing, it can be denied.

Unless you are prepared to respond within the 30 day period this could be the end of your claim, even though it is less than two years since the crime. I have no way of knowing what will occur if this happens to you, but I know that these words were intentionally included to warn you of the possibility of this denial.

Further, if you are not satisfied with the decision of the Division as to your eventual award, "you have 30 days from the date on the notice as to your award to WRITE to the Division to request a hearing to appeal the decision."

If you miss this date, your claim is over. Unlike the earlier 30 day requirement, which said it was the Divisions' *choice* to go on processing or stop, this one has no qualifying words which could allow you to continue the process. You miss the deadline and you are out, no if, ands or buts.

The bulletin continues with the following provisions which relate to time-frame situations: "The division will set a hearing date and notify you of time and location," and "Appeal hearings are held at the Violent Crime Compensation Division in INDIANAPOLIS." If you miss this hearing, your claim is over.

And finally: "The appeal hearing decision can be [further] appealed within 21 days to the Division Director. All further appeals would be to the State Court of Appeals." Now if you don't like the results of your hearing appeal, you have only a very short time (21 days) to appeal to the director. No qualifying language. If you miss the deadline, it's all over. This is the general rule and not the exception. You will find this problem in every state. Dates are serious and you must pay strict attention to them.

Chapter 11
Filing Your Claim

Make certain the crime has been reported to the police. If you are not sure it has been reported, report it yourself. Then obtain a copy of the police report and make yourself a copy of the report.

Next, obtain an application form from the commission. You will find a complete list of all the states as well as the District of Columbia and the Virgin Islands in this book. The list includes everything you need to know in order to obtain your application forms. When you call them, or write to them, be sure to ask them to send you any brochures or information they think will be helpful.

In addition, find out if anyone in their department, or elsewhere, has been assigned the task of helping you if you encounter difficulty. In many jurisdictions, the county prosecutor's office will have application forms. Ask the commission to advise you. It may be more convenient if you can obtain your application forms locally.

Gather together and copy all necessary receipts before you submit your application. Remember the 30-day rule about completing your initial application or supplying them with any additional information they may request. Assemble your receipts and completed application, then either deliver the package to the commission office or mail it in. If you mail the package, remember to send it certified mail, return receipt requested. If you hand deliver the package, be sure to get a receipt.

Remember to sign the application, and don't forget any letters of explanation. They are especially important where you think your claim, either in part or in whole, requires additional explanation.

Follow through if you want your claim processed in a timely manner. First, obtain your claim number and always refer to this number in all your correspondence or telephone calls to the commission. Second, learn the name, telephone number, extension number and address of the person who is actually processing your claim.

There is an old saying which, unfortunately, applies here. "It is the squeaky wheel that gets oiled." Be polite but emphatic. The rule is be firm, fair and friendly. If you would like to get paid before the turn of the century, stay on top of the processing.

Ask the person who is processing your claim for a timetable. This will show you what is supposed to be happening and when it should happen. If at any time you make a request which you believe to be reasonable, and that request is denied, obtain the name of your processor's immediate supervisor. Don't be timid. If you have a problem or just a misunderstanding, contact the supervisor. Whether you believe this or not, everybody wants you to be paid.

No one is looking for fraud, however these processors constantly receive applications from well-meaning people who have no idea of what goes into the claim or the application. They will look at your application just like all of the rest they have processed.

Make sure the processor knows your telephone number, and understands what hours you can be contacted there. This helps keep the process going and insures that you will not trip over minor details. Encourage these calls. They are important. Calls work for you in both directions. Feel free to call and be called.

Whatever else you may do or not do, remember to ask the "$64,000.00 question," which is: When can I reasonably expect to get paid? It is your money. You are entitled to receive compensation. It is neither a gift or charity.

The program is funded through a combination of federal funds, (a grant from the United States Department of Justice), as well as a percentage of all court fees, work release moneys, restitution and trust funds collected state wide.

The next chapter will examine what the commission must do because you submitted an application.

Chapter 12
The Commission's Job

In Indiana, the board which administers the crime victim compensation program is called, "The Violent Crime Compensation Division." For our purposes, we will refer to them as the "commission." Upon receipt of your claim, the commission will establish a file and claim number. In addition, they may make a temporary estimate as to the size of your claim.

They will review your application according to the order in which is was received. Obviously, there are a lot of claims. It is their obligation to investigate your claim. They are trying to verify the truth of the information you provided in your application.

Once they are satisfied as to the truth of your claim, they will turn to the accuracy of your statements. This is all part of the process of determining the extent of your loss. It is possible that you got everything right and complete on your first try. But if the commission says you did not, then this is what happens next.

The commission may tell you that your application is not properly completed. They could also advise you that additional information is required.

In either case, the commission must send you a written explanation of what is needed. Again, you have only 30 days to deal with their request.

Finally, the commission must notify you by mail as to the results of the commission's investigation and their decision. The commission may make an award in full, in part, or deny the claim altogether.

If the total amount of the claim exceeds the limitation, commonly known as the cap, the commission will proportionally divide the award among the providers. This means, in English, everybody gets something, but no one gets everything they claimed. Everyone gets paid the same percentage.

Chapter 13
When Will You Get Your Money?

This question has been included as part of this discussion because of its obvious importance. The sad thing about this question is there is no specific answer. Actually, this is the wrong question to ask.

The right question to should ask is: Why would I not be paid? The answer to that question is simple. You will not be paid if you do not file. You will not be paid if you file incorrectly. You will not be paid if you file incompletely.

If you file correctly and completely, you will be paid shortly thereafter. However long it takes, it will be sooner rather than later, if you do a good job and follow through. Remember, the squeaky wheel gets oiled first.

If you are not satisfied with this answer, and I would not be satisfied, call the commission. Perhaps they know the answer and will be willing to share it with you. When I called, I was told that payment usually occurs within sixty to ninety days after a complete review. That answer implies that everything goes according to plan.

Chapter 14
Appeals

Everybody wants you to be satisfied as much as is possible within the limits stated by the act. Chances are you will be satisfied, but what do you do if you are not? You have the right to appeal.

Sometimes, it is wise to consider the obvious. How much do you think you can gain above and beyond what you have already been told you will receive? Ask your commission how long the appeal process might take? Even if you are successful in your appeal, how much additional time will it take before you get your money? Weigh the options and decide if you want to appeal.

For the sake of this discussion, let us assume you have decided to appeal. Once again for an example, we turn to the rules as they now exist in Indiana. As things stand, you must file your appeal no later than thirty days from the date of the notice you received describing your award.

Your request must be in writing, addressed to the commission. You must state that you wish to appeal the decision initially rendered by the commission. In effect, you are asking one part of an administrative tribunal to reverse the decision of another part of the same tribunal. Obviously, you mail your request utilizing certified mail, return receipt requested.

The commission will set a hearing date and notify you in writing as to the time and location. In Indiana, appeal hearings are held at the Violent Crime Compensation Division in Indianapolis. This, however, is not necessarily the end of the appellate process.

If you receive the decision of the division on your appeal, and you are still not satisfied, you have additional options available to you. You can, if you desire, climb further up the appellate ladder and appeal directly to the Director of the Violent Crime Compensation Division

With this appeal, you have less time. The procedure is simple. You write the Director and advise his office as to your decision to appeal one more time. This time you have only 21 days to complete the process. Once more, mail your request, "certified mail, return receipt requested."

What you have just gone through is known in the law as, "the doctrine of exhaustion of administrative remedies." If you are still not satisfied, you can leave the familiar halls of the Violent Crime Compensation Division and appeal to the State Court of Appeals.

If you do file an appeal, you are now dealing with a concept that can operate against you. Your act of requesting a hearing is the same as saying, "I acknowledge the fact that you decided against me in part or in whole and that your decision, as far as you are concerned, is final."

There is one other possibility available to you, although it will not have any effect on the fact that you only have 30 days in which to request an appeal hearing. This possibility resembles a legal procedure, which is usually called, a "motion for reconsideration."

In law, if you are not satisfied with the court's decision, prior to any appeal, you may ask the court to reconsider their decision. If your motion is refused [denied], you may still appeal to another court, generally a court of appeals. If your motion for reconsideration is granted, and the court does not change it's original opinion, then you still have your appeal.

Most states do not provide any procedure for reconsideration but nothing says you cannot ask the commission to do this.

If you attempt this on your own, remember, no matter what you are told, the 30-day clock is ticking as to your need to request a hearing for a proper, statutory-authorized appeal. You must write the commission and request a hearing to appeal the decision. Again, remember to use certified mail, return receipt requested.

Chapter 15
Where To Find Help

Court Appeals and Lawyers

An appeal to a court is probably the end of your non-lawyer days. Unless you are prepared to spend countless hours at the law library studying law and appellate procedure, and withstand pressure from judges, lawyers and court clerks, you should be represented by an attorney. This costs serious dollars. Up until now the decision was win money now or perhaps win greater but later. Now for the first time, you could also lose money, by having to pay lawyers fees and court costs.

You could call the state bar association and find out if any member will represent you without charging you a fee. This would be based upon your relative inability to pay a fee and the compassion of a state bar member willing to come to your assistance.

Some courts permit representation by a senior law school student under special circumstances. Call the State Court of Appeals and ask the Court Clerk if such representation would be permitted. If so, all you have left to do is call the nearest law school and ask them for assistance.

Do not be overly concerned about the fact that your legal advocate is a student. No one knows more law than a law student about to take the state bar examination for the very first time. Since the student normally cannot determine what questions will be on the bar examination, he or she must be prepared for anything and the word anything includes your relatively simple appeal. If you cannot get a "free" attorney or a law student, you still have one more option. Start calling attorneys and ask them if they are willing to represent you on the following fee basis.

Tell them that all you can afford to pay is whatever the division is willing to award you as legal fees. Tell them that you will authorize direct payment to them. As we have already stated, this amount generally will be from ten percent to fifteen percent of the total recovery.

The Indiana Violent Crime Compensation Division sums up the issue of legal representation as follows:

It is not necessary to have an attorney to apply for Violent Crime Compensation or to appeal a decision of the Division.

However, if you choose to have an attorney and receive an award from the fund, reasonable attorney fees may be paid by Violent Crime Compensation.

Other Types of Assistance

Aside from hiring a lawyer, there are other types of assistance and support available.

You can call either the Commission or your prosecutor and find out if there is a victims' support or advocacy group in your area. If there is, call them and do not be shy about asking them for their assistance. They are dedicated to the task of helping you. In addition, they are well-experienced and probably know the "local ropes." This is a time and a society that has become aware of victims' rights. There will never be a better time or climate to assert your rights.

Some state have appointed persons to come to your aid. These representatives are called "ombudsmen."

Ombudsmen are your advocates before the system. Their only job is to advise you of your rights and to facilitate your effort to gain compensation for your losses. In those jurisdictions where no ombudsman program exists, help is still readily available through the offices of victim support groups.

The following information is supplied through the National Institute of Justice in their publication entitled, *Victims of Crime, an Overview*. There is no publication date provided.

The National Victims Resource Center includes a database containing the names, addresses and descriptions of more that 1,400 victims' assistance programs nationwide."

A partial list of such groups includes the following:

Center for Women Policy Studies
2000 P Street, NW Suite 508
Washington, DC 20036
(202) 872-1770

Parents of Murdered Children
National Headquarters
100 E. St. B-41
Cincinnati, OH 45202
(513) 721-5683

Mothers Against Drunk Drivers (MADD)
National Headquarters
511 E. John Carpenter Freeway, Suite 700
Irving, TX 75062
(214) 744-6233

National District Attorneys Association
1033 North Fairfax Street, Suite 200
Alexandria, VA 22314
(703) 549-9222

National Organization for Victim Assistance (NOVA)
1757 Park Road, NW
Washington, DC 20010
(202) 232-6682

National Victims Resource Center (NVRC)
P.O. BOX 6000
Rockville, MD 20850
(800) 627-6872

Students Against Driving Drunk (SADD)
National headquarters
250 Pleasant Street
P.O. BOX 800
Marlboro, MA 01752

National Victim Center
307 7th Street, Suite 1001
Fort Worth, TX 76102
(817) 877-3355

Chapter 16
Restitution

There are other ways for victims to obtain compensation when the victims fund is either unavailable, inappropriate, or inadequate. The best known, and most often used, of these alternatives is "restitution." This is where the court orders a convicted defendant to pay the victim for the victim's loss.

Restitution differs from the victims compensation fund in two important ways: First, there must be a conviction because restitution is a court ordered sanction or penalty against a convicted defendant. Second, there is usually no guarantee that the defendant has funds or assets from which the victim can automatically collect.

What gives this remedy teeth is that the judge can make restitution a requirement of probation and, of course, every defendant wants probation. If the defendant fails to make restitution his or her probation can be revoked.

State legislatures have expressly established restitution as an appropriate post-conviction remedy. While this remedy has been in existence for a long time, it was seldom used until recent times.

The rapid increase in the rate of violent crime, together with pressure from victims rights groups, has renewed interest in restitution. As a result, courts have dramatically increased the use of restitution as a postconviction sanction. Most of the states which have either recognized or authorized this sanction permit the judge to decide whether or not to require restitution.

Modern state laws have taken three other, and different, directions as to the ultimate degree of discretion allowed the court. In addition to the complete discretion mentioned above, some state have taken different directions. First, some state laws make restitution mandatory in certain cases. Second, some states require consideration of the possibility of restitution as a prior condition to probation. Third, other states require the court to formally state it's reasons for not ordering restitution. That means, of course, the court must put it's reasons in writing.

The same holds true of parole boards. The difference is that the court can choose to order restitution prior to incarceration as a way to avoid jail, while parole boards can offer restitution after incarceration as a way of obtaining early release from jail. Both the courts and the parole boards consider the apparent ability of the defendant to pay restitution. Enforcing restitution orders is difficult at best. It is also costly to the state which imposed the sanction. Too often the defendant is poor, or chooses to defy the court and gets away with it.

Chapter 17
"Son of Sam" Laws

The notorious killer who was nicknamed, "Son of Sam," stalked the streets of New York creating a reign of terror. In 1977, he sold the literary rights to his story for approximately $200,000 dollars.

The public became outraged over this event and state legislatures went to work. The states quickly enacted laws which enabled victims to reach out and seize those ill-gotten gains. This has become an additional source of compensation for victims of violent crime.

The legislation provides that funds created by the publicity arising from the criminal activity be paid directly into an escrow fund managed by the state. Victims are given regular notice of the existence of this fund. If the victim is successful in obtaining a civil judgment against the criminal (by way of a lawsuit), the victim can recover from this fund.

Any funds unclaimed, after a given period of time, are paid directly into the state's victim compensation fund.

If you have any problems or difficulty accessing these funds, contact the Victims of Violent Crime Fund administrator for your area, the ombudsman, or a crime victim advocate group.

Chapter 18
Your Other Rights

While the purpose of this book is to enumerate your rights in the area of compensation, it is important for you to realize there are also non-compensatory rights available to victims and claimants. Victims can use these additional rights as a way to get involved in the prosecution, and, hopefully, the sentencing of wrong-doers.

This chapter will provide a brief description and summary of these additional rights. While they do not provide compensation, they can provide much needed satisfaction to the victims and their families. This discussion begins with a brief list of the problems that victims and related claimants faced prior to the enactment of these remedial laws. Of the many problems that existed, these are the ones most often referred to as causing the highest degree of dissatisfaction amongst the victims:

1. Intimidation of the victims, who fear the act of testifying in open court as well as fear the probability of bitter cross-examination by counsel for the defense.

2. Fear of law enforcement personnel because they might accuse the victim of inciting the crime and of participation in that crime. The victims also fear the possibility of being accused of tacitly allowing the crime to occur.

3. Fear of reprisal by the accused if the victim cooperates with the authorities due to the lack of proper police protection.

4. Well-founded concern over the possibility that the defendant will receive little or no punishment as a result of prosecutorial plea-bargaining.

5. Fear of wasting time, and the resulting loss of wages, by victims who come to the criminal's trial and are put off time after time by unwarranted continuances.

6. Anxiety as to the prospect of unreasonable delays in the return of their personal property being held as evidence for trial.

7. Problems in obtaining child care, transportation and parking, which often keep victims from attending court sessions.

8. Difficulty in obtaining information as to the progress of prosecution and sentencing, rendering participation by the victim nearly impossible.

9. Indifferent and often insensitive questioning by police and prosecutors, which fuels the victim's loss of self esteem and feelings of violation and humiliation which are the results of being victimized.

The criminal justice system could be, at least until now, characterized as offender-oriented. Modern federal and state legislation is rapidly changing our criminal justice system, and what is rapidly emerging is a new system which tends to be both offender- and victim-oriented. These new laws cluster around five areas of law which can be entitled:

1. Protection from intimidation.
2. Victim notification
3. Victim impact statements.
4. Employment relationships.
5. Third party advocates.

Protection From Intimidation

All states have existing provisions regarding obstruction of justice, witness tampering, and intimidation. In light of the epidemic rise in violent crime in general, and seemingly purposeless random violent crime in particular, these provisions are often found inadequate by the victims who would otherwise be witnesses.

Once again, fear is the operative word. Too many victims feel the protection offered to them if they testify, will not be adequate and, as a result, they do not come forward. Statistics verify this troubling state of affairs.

Some states have come to the realization that existing provisions of the law regarding victims' rights were inadequate to protect the victims and potential witnesses. As a result numerous changes in the law have taken place. They can be grouped as follows:

1. Laws which authorize an increase in the number and kind of acts deemed to be intimidating.

2. Laws which authorize a broad increase in the class of persons protected by these laws.

3. Laws which authorize the criminal courts to issue a wide range of protective orders further safeguarding the victims and potential witnesses.

This strategy has been, at best, only partially successful. Current data demonstrates an increase in victim participation in the criminal justice system, but the over-all gain in participation as compared to the rise in crime is totally unacceptable.

Victim Notification

No matter how exemplary the programs enacted for the benefit of victims may be, they are all but useless if the victims are unaware of their existence. Random violent crime most often affects those in our society who are least likely to be aware of programs which were put in place for their protection and assistance. Thus notification is a crucial and vital part of these programs.

Most states have a notification program making various state and local officials, usually prosecutors or police, responsible for notifying victims as to the existence of a program operating on their behalf. The assumption is that they will make first contact with the victim following the perpetration of the crime. In addition, medical personnel in emergency rooms are also trained in the process of victim notification.

Compensation programs require the victim to cooperate with police and prosecutors alike. You would think that this is certainly sufficient to guarantee notification but that has not been the case until now. The results of this systematic approach to notification have been dismal at best. The root of the problem lies with the failure on the part of our authorities to understand the negative state of mind of the victims. Far too often, the victims feel that any attempt at cooperation on their part is either useless or downright dangerous. In addition to official lack of understanding, lies the fact that, far too often, the officials fail to create any positive programs to overcome that negativity. There is a crying need for psychological counseling for victims the moment officials become aware of their victimization.

There is a duty to notify the victim as to the existence of a program of compensation which may cover his or her loss. There is a further duty to keep the victim informed as to the progress of the criminal case. The victim must be constantly appraised as to the current status of the criminal case as well as to all postponements. This is a significant additional burden placed on already over-burdened prosecutorial personnel.

The victim must be made aware of the right to be heard at sentencing. The victim has a right to be heard at all parole hearings including the release of the offender from custody. Some states require that the victim be informed of all attempts at plea bargaining. The victim may comment on all attempts by the defense to include the offender in a pre-trial intervention program which could lighten the sentence about to be imposed upon the offender.

Victim Impact Statements

This discussion now turns to what the victims can do relative to the prosecution of the criminal case against the offender. They can create and forward to the court what is called a victim impact statement. This is the victim's day in court. A victim impact statement describes the impact the crime has had in their lives which is almost always negative.

At last count, thirty-three states have enacted laws permitting this statement to be heard by the judge. The victim impact statement is usually included in the presentencing report. The victim usually has the right to submit a written statement to any parole boards, and in some states the victim may be allowed to appear before the parole board and be heard by the members of that board.

The same rules apply to plea bargaining although it is usually more difficult to sway the opinion of the prosecutor who is dealing with a major case load. He is usually quick to plea bargain as it is his best method of alleviating a backlog of cases. Still, the right exists and it is prudent, if you are a victim, to stay abreast of the developments. Remember, the judge can turn down a negotiated plea bargain if he deems it to be in everyone's best interest, and the term, "everyone," now includes the victim. These rules also apply where the defendant seeks admission to a pre-trial admission program. These are special programs designed to keep the offender from being tried in criminal cases.

Typical of these programs are youthful offender programs or perhaps special programs for first offenders. The idea is that the offender has made a tragic mistake but perhaps could still be rehabilitated rather than incarcerated.

This is the compassionate side of justice in operation, but justice can only be served when the rights of victims are given just as much protection as those of the defendant. It is hoped that the victim impact statement can contribute to that desired balance.

A few states go much further and permit the victim to hire a private attorney. Theoretically, that attorney can assist the prosecutor in fact gathering and prosecution. This is important in a case where the prosecutor is over-powered by a well-paid defense lawyer with an equally well-paid investigative staff. These lawyers have reputations that precede them into the courtroom. The victim's privately financed attorney often serves to even up the playing field.

He knows how to properly utilize the victim impact statement as a means of convincing the court to reject any plea bargaining agreement. This is the best guarantee that exists of the victim's right to be heard by the court in a meaningful fashion.

Employment Relationships

Repeated absence from work by the victim due to multiple court appearances can, and often does, cause friction in the work place. Too many employers care little or nothing about the trauma placed upon the victim, and threaten the victim with loss of employment or other sanctions. This moved many states into enactment of laws designed to protect victims from discrimination at the job site.

The mildest of these laws encourages officials to explain to employers the need for absences on the part of the victim because of court appearances. If that does not succeed in curing the problem, the laws get more stringent.

There are many sanctions which can be used against the employer in an effort to change his attitude. Perhaps the most effective measure is the power to levy fines against an obstinate employer who is not moved by a succession of less stringent penalties. However, it is important to realize that employers have rights and needs, and these needs must be considered in the imposition of any sanctions.

The key here, as in all instances involving human dynamics, is balance. Balance is learned through experience, and experience is gained through a process known as trial and error. We are far from perfect and we leave that imperfect imprint on the systems we create. Chief among those imperfect systems is our judicial system, but it is encouraging to note that momentum is swinging in the direction of the victims.

Third-Party Advocates

Some states have passed laws establishing and funding support personnel to come to the aid of the victim and to assist the victim though the judicial process. They are sometimes called, "ombudsmen." They clearly have the right to be present in court and receive information about the defendant which would be otherwise privileged and not available for publication to an uninvolved third-party.

Unfortunately, there is a problem forthird-party advocate groups like Mothers Against Drunk Drivers (MADD) which often wish to take part in the judicial process. They have no legally recognized right to participate in those proceedings. Still, they make their presence felt by all involved.

Many a judge has looked out on a sea of angry faces on sentencing day as he considered the fate of a convicted drunken driver. Sentences harden under their watchful presence, especially in states where judges are elected. Perhaps these advocate groups should be included in the criminal justice system, but constitutional guarantees as to the right of privacy on the behalf of the defendant makes their inclusion difficult, if not impossible as a matter of law.

Summary

Traditionally, the criminal justice system has always been played out by only two sides, prosecution and defense. It was really a three player game all this time, but for some reason, the victim went unnoticed, and for the most part, unrepresented. As random, violent crime sweeps our country, this state of affairs is no longer acceptable. As we change, our systems must change as well.

The rules have changed and it is time to let our populace become aware of these changes. Foremost in the area of victims rights is the right to compensation. Until such time as we learn how to abate these violent acts, at the very least, we can alleviate much of the suffering they cause.

Appendix A
Application Checklist

This appendix contains a summary checklist of various things to consider and review when filing a claim. This list is not necessarily comprehensive, but is designed to serve as a quick reference and review.

When pursuing your claim be certain that:

1. You file for benefits in the state where the crime occurred.

2. The crime which has caused your loss is either a felony or a misdemeanor which resulted in bodily injury or death to the victim (or property damage if allowed in your state). If you have any doubt, check with the commission.

3. The crime has been immediately reported to the authorities. Obtain a copy of that report so that you can prove it if necessary.

4. The victim did not engage in any conduct which contributed to the occurrence of the crime. Be prepared to debate this where either alcohol or drugs were present at the scene of the crime

5. You suffered at least one hundred dollars in out of pocket expenses.

6. You file your application for benefits within the time allowed with plenty of time to spare for additional questions and requests for additional information if requested. Remember you have only thirty days for each separate request from the commission.

7. You have gathered every receipt before you file. Determine whether you must submit those receipts with your initial application. If you still are in doubt, submit them. Remember to make and keep copies of everything you submit.

8. You have completed every blank space on the application form. Remember to attach narrative explanations of any items you consider to be unusual or ambiguous. If you have any doubts, submit them.

9. You are permitted to submit any charge for attorneys fees. Those fees should not exceed 15% of the proposed total settlement. 10% is always safe where permitted. Both the inclusion of attorneys fees and the percentage allowed must be determined and complied with before filing for them. Your commission will answer these questions for you.

10. You either file your applications and proofs in person or if you choose to file by mail, make it certified mail, return receipt requested. If you file in person, be sure and get a detailed receipt.

11. All collateral sources of reimbursement have been exhausted and reported to the commission before any final award is made. This fund is considered to be a "payer of last resort." If you collect from any other source after you receive your award, and this latter payment duplicates any part of your award, you must pay the duplicated portion back to the fund.

12. You comply with all of the deadlines previously mentioned in this book. This is especially important if you utilize the appeals provisions.

13. If you do not fall into a typical category of claimants, you carefully explain your particular set of circumstances that make you an appropriate candidate for reimbursement. For example: You are not the parents of the victim, but you are the legal guardians.

14. You can prove any special relationship or unusual claim. In the example cited above, you would submit articles or letters of legal guardianship to establish your claim. In this case, the expenses you claim must be as reimbursement for those expenses your role as legal guardian required you to accept and pay.

A second example would be that of a claimant with a normal relationship but suffering an unusual financial loss. An example of this would be the husband of a spouse who was raped. Certainly, she could require psychological counseling as a direct result of the crime committed upon her person, but perhaps, her husband is just as much a victim of her assault. Counseling programs for both of them are often suggested and implemented under the auspices of the fund. Whatever the particular circumstances of your particular claim, a good guideline would be, "if you file, be prepared to prove your claim."

Appendix B
Crime Compensation
Agencies

This list is supplied through the courtesy of The National Association of Crime Victims Boards, P.O. Box 16003, Alexandria, Virginia.

ALABAMA

Anita A. Drummond, Executive Director
Crime Victims Compensation Commission
P.O. Box 1548
Montgomery, AL 36102-1548

Tel. (205) 242-4007

ALASKA

Nola K. Capp, Administrator
Violent Crimes Compensation Board
P.O. Box 111200
Juneau, AK 99811

Tel. (907) 465-3040

ARIZONA

Rita Yorke,Victims Service Coordinator
Criminal Justice Commission
1501 West Washington, Suite 207
Phoenix, AZ 85007

Tel. (602) 542-1928

ARKANSAS

Ginger Bailey, Director
Crime Victims Reparations Board
Office of the Attorney General
601 Tower Bldg. 323 Center St.
Little Rock, AR 72201

Tel. (501) 682-1323

CALIFORNIA

Ted Boughton, Deputy Director
Victims of Crime Program
P.O. Box 3036
Sacramento, CA 95812-3036

Tel. (916) 323-6251

COLORADO

Bob Bush, Criminal Justice Specialist
Division of Criminal Justice
700 Kipling St., Suite 3000
Denver, CO 80215

Tel. (303) 271-6840

CONNECTICUT

Anne Menard, Director
Commission on Victim Services
1155 Silas Deane Highway
Wethersfield, CT 06109

Tel. (203) 529-3089

DELAWARE

Ed Stansky, Executive Secretary
Violent Crimes Compensation Board
1500 E. Newport Pike, Suite 10
Wilmington, DE 19804

Tel. (302) 995-8383

DISTRICT OF COLUMBIA

Joan Watson, Acting Director
Crime Victims Compensation Program
Department of Employment Services
1200 Upshur St., N.W.
Washington, DC 20011

Tel. (202) 576-7706

FLORIDA

Meg Bates, Director
Division of Victim Services
Office of Attorney General
The Capitol PL-01
Tallahassee, FL 32399-1050

Tel. (904) 488-0848

GEORGIA
John C. Wise, Program Director
Crime Victim Compensation Program
Criminal Justice Coordination Council
503 Oak Place South, Suite 540
Atlanta, GA 30349

Tel. (404) 559-4949

HAWAII
Estre Quilausing, Administrator
Criminal Injuries Compensation Commission
335 Merchant Street, Suite 244
Honolulu, HI 96813-2907

Tel. (808) 587-1143

IDAHO
[vacant] Director
Victim Compensation Program
Idaho Industrial Commission
317 Main Street
Boise, ID 83720

Tel. (208) 334-6000

ILLINOIS
David Ubell, Deputy Chief
Crimes Victims Division
Office of the Attorney General
100 W. Randolph, 13th floor
Chicago, IL 60601

Tel. (312) 814-2581

Bob Westbrook, Fiscal Officer
Illinois Court of Claims
630 South College
Springfield, IL 62756

Tel. (217) 782-0703

INDIANA
Kay Carter, Hearing Officer
Violent Crimes Victim
Compensation Bureau
402 W. Washington St., Rm. W-382
Indianapolis, IN 46204

Tel. (317) 232-3809

IOWA
Kelly Brodie, Deputy Administrator
Crime Victim Assistance Program
Department of Justice
Old Historical Building
Des Moines, IA 50319

Tel. (515) 281-5044

KANSAS
Betty Bomar, Director
Crime Victims Reparations Board
700 S.W. Jackson, Suite 400
Topeka, KS 66603-3741

Tel. (913) 296-2359

KENTUCKY
Jackie Howell, Director
Crime Victims Compensation Board
115 Myrtle Ave.
Frankfort, KY 40601

Tel. (502) 564-2290

LOUISIANA
Rosanna Hollingsworth, Manager
Crime Victims Reparation Board
1885 Wooddale Blvd. Suite 708
Baton Rouge, LA 70806

Tel. (504) 925-4437

MAINE
Jeanette Hagen
Crime Victim Compensation Program
Office of the Attorney General
State House Station #6
Augusta, ME 04333

Tel. (207) 626-8589

MARYLAND
Esther Scaljon, Director
Criminal Injuries Compensation Board
6776 Reisterstown Road Suite 313
Baltimore, MD 21215-2340

Tel. (410) 764-4214

MASSACHUSETTS
[vacant] Chief
Victims Compensation and Assistance
Office of the Attorney General
One Ashburton Place
Boston, MA 02108

Tel. (617) 727-2300, ext. 2875

MICHIGAN
Michael J. Fullwood, Administrator
Crime Victims Compensation Board
P.O. Box 30026
Lansing, MI 48909

Tel. (517) 373-7373

MINNESOTA
Mary Ellison, Executive Director
Crime Victims Reparations Board
1821 University Ave. N465
St. Paul, MN 55104

Tel. (612) 642-0395

MISSISSIPPI
Sandra Morrison, Hearing Officer
Crime Victim Compensation Program
P.O. Box 267
Jackson, MS 39205

Tel. (800) 829-6766

MISSOURI
Connie Souden, Supervisor
Crime Victims Compensation Unit
Department of Labor and Industrial Relations
P.O. Box 58
Jefferson City, MO 65102

Tel. (314) 525-6006

MONTANA
Cheryl Bryant, Administrative Officer
Crime Victims Unit, Board of Crime Control
303 N. Roberts, 4th floor
Helena, MT 59620-1408

Tel. (406) 444-3653

NEBRASKA
Nancy Steeves, Federal Aid Administrator
Commission on Law Enforcement
P.O. Box 94946
Lincoln, NE 68509

Tel. (402) 471-2828

NEVADA
Bryan Nix, Coordinator
Victims of Crime Program
2770 Maryland Parkway
Suite 416
Las Vegas, NV 89109

Tel. (702) 486-7259

Gina Crown, Compensation Officer
40 W. 1st St.
Room 222
Reno, NV 89501

Tel. (702) 688-2900

NEW HAMPSHIRE
Mark, Thompson, Director of Administration
Tara Bickford Bailey, Coordinator
Victims Compensation Program
Department of Justice
State House Annex
Concord, NH 03301-6397

Tel. (603)271-1284

NEW JERSEY
Jacob Toporek, Chairman
Violent Crimes Compensation Board
60 Park Place, Suite 10
Newark, NJ 07102

Tel. (201) 648-2107

NEW MEXICO
Larry Tackman, Director
Crime Victims Reparations Commission
8100 Mountain Road N.E., Suite 106
Albuquerque, NM 87110-7822

Tel. (505) 841-9432

NEW YORK
Barbara Leak, Chairperson
Crime Victims Board
270 Broadway, Room 200
New York, NY 10007

Tel. (212) 417-5133

Lorraine Felegy, Commissioner
845 Central Ave.
Albany, NY 12206

Tel. (518) 457-8001

NORTH CAROLINA
Gary Eichelberger, Director
Victim and Justice Services
Department of Crime Control and Public Safety
P.O. Box 27687
Raleigh, NC 27611-7687

Tel. (919) 733-7974

NORTH DAKOTA
Paul Coughlin, Administrator
Crime Victim Reparations Program
Division of Parole and Probation
Box 5521
Bismark, ND 58502=5521

Tel. (701) 221-6195

OHIO

John Annarino, Director
Victims of Crime Compensation Program
Court of Claims of Ohio
65 E. State St. Suite 1100
Columbus, OH 43215

Tel. (614) 466-7190

Sally Cooper, Chief
Crime Victim Services
Office of the Attorney General
30 East Broad Street, 26th Fl.
Columbus, OH 43266-0410

Tel. (614) 466-5610

OKLAHOMA

Suzanne Breedlove, Director of Victim Services
Crime Victims Compensation Board
2200 Classen Blvd., Suite 1800
Oklahoma City, OK 73106-5811

Tel. (405) 557-6704

OREGON

Gerri J. Badden, Director
Crime Victims Assistance Section
Department of Justice
100 Justice Building
Salem, OR 97310

Tel. (503) 378-5348

PENNSYLVANIA
Marianne F. McManus, Board Chairman
Crime Victims' Compensation Board
333 Market Street
Lobby Level
Harrisburg, PA 17191

Tel. (717) 783-5153

RHODE ISLAND
Robert J. Melucci, State Coordinator
Judicial Planning Section
Supreme Court
250 Benefit Street
Providence, RI 02903

Tel. (401) 277-2500

Steve Palmer, Chief of Staff
Office of the General Treasurer
State House, Room 102
Providence, RI 02903

Tel. (401) 277-2397

SOUTH CAROLINA
[vacant], Director
Governor's Office
Division of Victim Assistance
P.O. Box 210009
Columbia, SC 29221-0009

Tel. (803) 737-8142

SOUTH DAKOTA
Emilia (Mimi) Olson, Exec. Director
Crime Victims' Compensation Commission
Department of Corrections
115 East Dakota Ave.
Pierre, SD 57501-3216

Tel. (605) 773-3478

TENNESSEE
Susan Clayton, Director
Division of Claims Administration
11th Floor, Volunteer Plaza
Andrew Jackson Building
Nashville, TN 37243-0243

Tel. (615) 741-2734

TEXAS
Mine Epps, Director
Richard Anderson, Assistant Director
Crime Victims Compensation Division
Office of the Attorney General
P.O. Box 12548, Capitol Station
Austin, TX 78711-2548

Tel. (512) 462-6400

UTAH
Dan R. Davis, Director
Office of Crime Victim Reparations
350 East 500 South, Suite 200
Salt Lake City, UT 84111

Tel. (801) 533-4000

VERMONT
Patricia Hayes, Executive Director
Vermont Center for Crime Victim Services
P.O. Box 991
Montpelier, VT 05601

Tel. (802) 828-3374

VIRGIN ISLANDS
Ruth D. Smith, Administrator
Crime Victims Compensation Commission
1303 Hospital Ground
Charlotte Amalie, VI 00802

Tel. (809) 774-1166

VIRGINIA
Robert Armstrong, Director
Crime Victims Compensation Division
P.O. Box 5423
Richmond, VA 23220

Tel. (804) 367-8686

WASHINGTON
Richard Ervin, Program Manager
Crime Victim Compensation Program
Department of Labor and Industries
P.O. Box 44520
Olympia, WA 98504-4520

Tel. (206) 956-5340

WEST VIRGINIA
Cheryle M. Hall, Clerk
Court of Claims, Crime Victim Compensation
Building 1, Room 6
1900 Kanawha Blvd., East
Charleston, WV 25305-0291

Tel. (304) 558-3471

WISCONSIN
Carol Latham, Executive Director
Office of Crime Victim Services
Office of Attorney General
P.O. Box 7951
Madison, WI 53707-7951

Tel. (608) 266-6470

WYOMING
Sylvia Bagdonas, Director
Crime Victims Compensation Commission
1700 Westland Rd.
Cheyenne, WY 82002

Tel. (307) 635-4050

Appendix C
State-By-State Summary
Of Laws

Some of the following material was obtained from The National Institute of Justice. The material can be found in their publication entitled, *Compensating Crime Victims: A Summary of Policies and Benefits*. Other information was obtained from individual state pamphlets. The author expresses his gratitude to The National Institute of Justice for this meaningful contribution.

These rules occasionally change. Check within your own prosecutor for a current update. Generally speaking, changes which have occurred usually operate in your favor.

Alabama

Persons eligible: injured party, spouse, children, parents, siblings

Compensable crimes:

Assault and battery	Motor vehicle crime
Child physical abuse	Rape
Child sexual abuse	Robbery
Domestic abuse	Sex offenses
Drunk driving	Spouse abuse
Homicide	

Maximum Award: $10,000

Emergency Funds: $500

Time limit for reporting crime: 3 days

Time limit for filing application: 1 year

Processing time for filing application: 16 weeks

Processing time for emergency funds: 2 days

Time limit for first appeal: 30 days

Method of payment: lump sum/direct to vendor

Compensable losses
    Medical: $10,000
    Mental health counseling: $5,000
    Disability/Loss of earnings: $5,200
    Rehabilitation: $10,000
    Funeral: $3,000
    Attorney fees: No
    Replacement services: $10,000
    Pain and suffering: No
    Property loss: $500

Fine print: Contributory conduct can reduce your claim

Note: These laws change frequently. Check with the prosecutor for any changes which affect your case.

Alaska

Persons eligible: injured party, spouse, children, parents, siblings

Compensable crimes:

Child physical abuse	Motor vehicle crime
Child sexual abuse	Rape
Domestic abuse	Robbery
Drunk driving	Sex offenses
Homicide	Spouse abuse

Maximum Award: $40,000

Emergency Funds: $1,500

Time limit for reporting crime: 5 days

Time limit for filing application: 2 years

Processing time for filing application: 16 weeks

Processing time for emergency funds: 3 days

Time limit for first appeal: 30 days

Method of payment: lump sum/installments

Compensable losses
  Medical: $1,000
  Mental health counseling: $1,000
  Disability/Loss of earnings: $1,000
  Rehabilitation: $1,000
  Funeral: $1,000
  Attorney fees: $1,000
  Replacement services: $1,000
  Pain and suffering: No
  Property loss: No

Fine print: Contributory conduct can reduce your claim

Note: These laws change frequently. Check with the prosecutor for any changes which affect your case.

Arizona

Persons eligible: injured party, spouse, children, parents, siblings

Compensable crimes:

Assault and battery	Homicide
Child physical abuse	Rape
Child sexual abuse	Robbery
Domestic abuse	Sex offenses
Drunk driving	Spouse abuse

Maximum Award: $10,000

Emergency Funds: $500

Time limit for reporting crime: 3 days

Time limit for filing application: 1 year

Processing time for filing application: 9 weeks

Processing time for emergency funds: 7 days

Time limit for first appeal: N/A

Method of payment: lump sum/installments/direct to vendors

Compensable losses
 Medical: $1,000
 Mental health counseling: $1,000; up to one year's
       expenses
 Disability/Loss of earnings: $1,000, up to $130/wk
 Rehabilitation: $1,000
 Funeral: $1,000
 Attorney fees: No
 Replacement services: $1,000
 Pain and suffering: No
 Property loss: No

Fine print: Contributory conduct can reduce your claim

Note: These laws change frequently. Check with the prosecutor for any changes which affect your case.

Arkansas

Persons eligible: injured party, spouse, children, parents, siblings

Compensable crimes:

Assault and battery	Motor vehicle crime
Child physical abuse	Rape
Child sexual abuse	Robbery
Domestic abuse	Sex offenses
Drunk driving	Spouse abuse
Homicide	

Maximum Award: $10,000

Emergency Funds: $500

Time limit for reporting crime: 3 days

Time limit for filing application: 1 year

Processing time for filing application: 10 weeks

Processing time for emergency funds: 22 days

Time limit for first appeal: 30 days

Method of payment: lump sum/installments/direct to vendors

Compensable losses
> **Medical:** $1,000
> **Mental health counseling:** $1,000
> **Disability/Loss of earnings:** $1,000
> **Rehabilitation:** $1,000
> **Funeral:** $1,000
> **Attorney fees:** No
> **Replacement services:** $1,000
> **Pain and suffering:** No
> **Property loss:** No

Fine print: Contributory conduct can reduce your claim

Note: These laws change frequently. Check with the prosecutor for any changes which affect your case.

California

Persons eligible: injured party, spouse, children, parents, siblings

Compensable crimes:

Assault and battery	Motor vehicle crime
Child physical abuse	Rape
Child sexual abuse	Robbery
Domestic abuse	Sex offenses
Drunk driving	Spouse abuse
Homicide	

Maximum Award: $6,000

Emergency Funds: $1,000

Time limit for reporting crime: N/A

Time limit for filing application: 1 year

Processing time for filing application: 40 weeks

Processing time for emergency funds: 30 days

Time limit for first appeal: 45 days

Method of payment: lump sum and/or direct to vendors

Compensable losses
    Medical: $1,000
    Mental health counseling: $1,000
    Disability/Loss of earnings: $10,000
    Rehabilitation: $1,000
    Funeral: $1,000
    Attorney fees: $500
    Replacement services: $1,000
    Pain and suffering: No
    Property loss: No

Fine print: Contributory conduct can reduce your claim

Note: These laws change frequently. Check with the prosecutor for any changes which affect your case.

Colorado

Persons eligible: families, secondary victims

Compensable crimes:

Assault and battery	Motor vehicle crime
Child physical abuse	Rape
Child sexual abuse	Robbery
Domestic abuse	Sex offenses
Drunk driving	Spouse abuse
Homicide	

Maximum Award: $10,000 Bodily injury or death; $250 repairs

Emergency Funds: $500

Time limit for reporting crime: 72 hours

Time limit for filing application: 1 year

Processing time for filing application: 2 weeks

Processing time for emergency funds: 1 day

Time limit for first appeal: varies

Method of payment: varies

Compensable losses
> **Medical:** reasonable
> **Mental health counseling:** varies
> **Disability/Loss of earnings:** varies
> **Rehabilitation:** varies
> **Funeral:** maximum determined locally
> **Attorney fees:** No
> **Replacement services:** locally determined
> **Pain and suffering:** No
> **Property loss:** $250

Fine print: Contributory conduct can reduce your claim

Note: These laws change frequently. Check with the prosecutor for any changes which affect your case.

Connecticut

Persons eligible: injured party, spouse, children, parents, siblings

Compensable crimes:

Assault and battery
Child physical abuse
Child sexual abuse
Domestic abuse
Drunk driving
Homicide

Motor vehicle crime
Rape
Robbery
Sex offenses
Spouse abuse

Maximum Award: $25,000

Emergency Funds: $500

Time limit for reporting crime: 5 days

Time limit for filing application: 2 years

Processing time for filing application: 13 weeks

Processing time for emergency funds: 1 day

Time limit for first appeal: 30 days

Method of payment: lump sum and/or to vendors

Compensable losses
Medical: $1,000
Mental health counseling: $1,000
Disability/Loss of earnings: $1,000
Rehabilitation: $1,000
Funeral: $1,000
Attorney fees: $1,000, up to 15% of total award
Replacement services: $1,000
Pain and suffering: No
Property loss: No

Fine print: Contributory conduct can reduce your claim

Note: These laws change frequently. Check with the prosecutor for any changes which affect your case.

Delaware

Persons eligible: injured party, spouse, children, parents, siblings

Compensable crimes:

Assault and battery	Motor vehicle crime
Child physical abuse	Rape
Child sexual abuse	Robbery
Domestic abuse	Sex offenses
Drunk driving	Spouse abuse
Homicide	

Maximum Award: $25,000

Emergency Funds: 0

Time limit for reporting crime: 3 days

Time limit for filing application: 1 year

Processing time for filing application: 13 weeks

Processing time for emergency funds: 2 days

Time limit for first appeal: 30 days

Method of payment: lump sum and/or to vendors

Compensable losses
Medical: $1,000
Mental health counseling: $1,000
Disability/Loss of earnings: $1,000
Rehabilitation: $1,000
Funeral: $1,000
Attorney fees: $1,000
Replacement services: $1,000
Pain and suffering: No
Property loss: No

Fine print: Contributory conduct can reduce your claim

Note: These laws change frequently. Check with the prosecutor for any changes which affect your case.

District of Columbia

Persons eligible: Injured party. Spouse, children, parents of victim when victim is killed.

Compensable crimes:

Assault and battery
Child physical abuse
Child sexual abuse
Domestic abuse
Drunk driving
Homicide

Motor vehicle crime
Rape
Robbery
Sex offenses
Spouse abuse

Maximum Award: $25,000

Emergency Funds: $1,000

Time limit for reporting crime: 7 days

Time limit for filing application: 180 days

Processing time for filing application: varies

Processing time for emergency funds: varies

Time limit for first appeal: 15 working days

Method of payment: direct to vendors

Compensable losses
Medical: Yes
Mental health counseling: Yes
Disability/Loss of earnings: Yes
Rehabilitation: yes
Funeral: $2,000
Attorney fees: No
Replacement services: Yes
Pain and suffering: No
Property loss: No

Fine print: Contributory conduct can reduce your claim

Note: These laws change frequently. Check with the prosecutor for any changes which affect your case.

Florida

Persons eligible: injured party, spouse, children, parents, siblings

Compensable crimes:

Assault and battery	Homicide
Child physical abuse	Rape
Child sexual abuse	Robbery
Drunk driving	Sex offenses

Maximum Award: $10,000

Emergency Funds: $500

Time limit for reporting crime: 3 days

Time limit for filing application: 1 year

Processing time for filing application: 16 weeks

Processing time for emergency funds: 15 days

Time limit for first appeal: 60 days

Method of payment: lump sum/installments/direct to vendors

Compensable losses
    Medical: $1,000
    Mental health counseling: $1,000
    Disability/Loss of earnings: $1,000
    Rehabilitation: $10,000
    Funeral: $1,000
    Attorney fees: No
    Replacement services: $10,000
    Pain and suffering: No
    Property loss: No

Fine print: Contributory conduct can reduce your claim

Note: These laws change frequently. Check with the prosecutor for any changes which affect your case.

Georgia

Persons eligible: injured party, spouse, children, parents, guardian, "Good Samaritan"

Compensable crimes:

Assault and battery	Domestic abuse
Child physical abuse	Homicide
Child sexual abuse	Motor vehicle crime

Maximum Award: $1,000

Emergency Funds: No

Time limit for reporting crime: 72 days

Time limit for filing application: 180 days

Processing time for filing application: 4 months

Processing time for emergency funds: 5 days

Time limit for first appeal: 30 days

Method of payment: lump sum and/or to vendors

Compensable losses
> **Medical:** actual expenses
> **Mental health counseling:** actual expenses
> **Disability/Loss of earnings:** actual expenses
> **Rehabilitation:** Yes
> **Funeral:** actual expenses
> **Attorney fees:** No
> **Replacement services:** N/A
> **Pain and suffering:** No
> **Property loss:** No

Fine print: Contributory conduct can reduce your claim

Note: These laws change frequently. Check with the prosecutor for any changes which affect your case.

Hawaii

Persons eligible: injured party, spouse, children, parents, siblings

Compensable crimes:

Assault and battery	Motor vehicle crime
Child physical abuse	Rape
Child sexual abuse	Robbery
Domestic abuse	Spouse abuse
Homicide	

Maximum Award: $10,000

Emergency Funds: No

Time limit for reporting crime: 18 months

Time limit for filing application: 18 months

Processing time for filing application: 40 weeks

Processing time for emergency funds: N/A

Time limit for first appeal: 30 days

Method of payment: lump sum and/or to vendors

Compensable losses
> **Medical:** $1,000
> **Mental health counseling:** $1,000
> **Disability/Loss of earnings:** $1,000
> **Rehabilitation:** $1,000
> **Funeral:** $1,000
> **Attorney fees:** 1,000, up to 15% of total award if total exceeds $1,000
> **Replacement services:** $1,000
> **Pain and suffering:** $1,000
> **Property loss:** $1,000

Fine print: Contributory conduct can reduce your claim

Note: These laws change frequently. Check with the prosecutor for any changes which affect your case.

Idaho

Persons eligible: injured party, spouse, children, parents, siblings

Compensable crimes:

Assault and battery	Motor vehicle crime
Child physical abuse	Rape
Child sexual abuse	Robbery
Domestic abuse	Sex offenses
Drunk driving	Spouse abuse
Homicide	

Maximum Award: $25,000

Emergency Funds: 0

Time limit for reporting crime: 3 days

Time limit for filing application: 1 year

Processing time for filing application: 9 weeks

Processing time for emergency funds: 10 days

Time limit for first appeal: 145 days

Method of payment: installments and/or direct to vendors

Compensable losses
    Medical: $2,500
    Mental health counseling: $1,000
    Disability/Loss of earnings: $1,000
    Rehabilitation: N/A
    Funeral: $1,000
    Attorney fees: 1,000, up to 5% of the total award
    Replacement services: $1,000
    Pain and suffering: No
    Property loss: No

Fine print: Contributory conduct can reduce your claim

Note: These laws change frequently. Check with the prosecutor for any changes which affect your case.

Illinois

Persons eligible: injured party

Compensable crimes:

Assault and battery	Homicide
Child physical abuse	Rape
Child sexual abuse	Sex offenses
Domestic abuse	Spouse abuse
Drunk driving	

Maximum Award: $25,000

Emergency Funds: No

Time limit for reporting crime: 1 year

Time limit for filing application: 1 year

Processing time for filing application: 6 months to 1 year

Processing time for emergency funds: N/A

Time limit for first appeal: 30 days

Method of payment: lump sumand/or to vendor

Compensable losses
  Medical: $25,000
  Mental health counseling: Yes
  Disability/Loss of earnings: $1,000/ month, pro rated
  Rehabilitation: Yes
  Funeral: $3,000
  Attorney fees: No
  Replacement services: Yes
  Pain and suffering: No
  Property loss: No

Fine print: Contributory conduct can reduce your claim

Note: These laws change frequently. Check with the prosecutor for any changes which affect your case.

Indiana

Persons eligible: injured party, spouse, children, parents, siblings

Compensable crimes:

Assault and battery	Homicide
Child physical abuse	Motor vehicle crime
Child sexual abuse	Rape
Domestic abuse	Sex offenses
Drunk driving	Spouse abuse
Homicide	

Maximum Award: $10,000

Emergency Funds: $500

Time limit for reporting crime: 2 days

Time limit for filing application: 2 years

Processing time for filing application: 7 weeks

Processing time for emergency funds: 2 days

Time limit for first appeal: 30 days

Method of payment: lump sum and/or installments

Compensable losses
   Medical: $10,000
   Mental health counseling: $10,000
   Disability/Loss of earnings: $10,000
   Rehabilitation: $10,000
   Funeral: $1,000
   Attorney fees: $1,250
   Replacement services: $10,000
   Pain and suffering: No
   Property loss: No

Fine print: Contributory conduct can reduce your claim

Note: These laws change frequently. Check with the prosecutor for any changes which affect your case.

114

Iowa

Persons eligible: injured party, spouse, children, parents, siblings

Compensable crimes:

Assault and battery	Motor vehicle crime
Child physical abuse	Rape
Child sexual abuse	Robbery
Domestic abuse	Sex offenses
Drunk driving	Spouse abuse
Homicide	

Maximum Award: $20,600

Emergency Funds: $500

Time limit for reporting crime: 7 days

Time limit for filing application: 1 year

Processing time for filing application: 16 weeks

Processing time for emergency funds: 2 days

Time limit for first appeal: 30 days

Method of payment: lump sum and/or to vendors

Compensable losses
Medical: $10,000
Mental health counseling: $500
Disability/Loss of earnings: $2,000
Rehabilitation: $1,000
Funeral: No
Attorney fees: $1,000
Replacement services: $1,000
Pain and suffering: No
Property loss: No

Fine print: Contributory conduct can reduce your claim

Note: These laws change frequently. Check with the prosecutor for any changes which affect your case.

Kansas

Persons eligible: injured party, spouse, children, parents

Compensable crimes:

Assault and battery	Homicide
Child physical abuse	Rape
Child sexual abuse	Sex offenses
Domestic abuse	Spouse abuse
Drunk driving	

Maximum Award: $10,000

Emergency Funds: 0

Time limit for reporting crime: 3 days

Time limit for filing application: 1 year

Processing time for filing application: 12 weeks

Processing time for emergency funds: N/A

Time limit for first appeal: 30 days

Method of payment: lump sum/installment/ direct to vendors

Compensable losses
Medical: $1,000
Mental health counseling: $1,000
Disability/Loss of earnings: $1,000
Rehabilitation: $1,000
Funeral: $1,000
Attorney fees: $1,000
Replacement services: $1,000
Pain and suffering: No
Property loss: No

Fine print: Contributory conduct can reduce your claim

Note: These laws change frequently. Check with the prosecutor for any changes which affect your case.

Kentucky

Persons eligible: injured party, spouse, children, parents, siblings

Compensable crimes:

Assault and battery	Homicide
Child physical abuse	Rape
Child sexual abuse	Sex offenses
Drunk driving	

Maximum Award: $25,000

Emergency Funds: $500

Time limit for reporting crime: 2 days

Time limit for filing application: 1 year

Processing time for filing application: 20 weeks

Processing time for emergency funds: 30 days

Time limit for first appeal: 30 days

Method of payment: lump sum/installments/direct to vendors

Compensable losses
Medical: $25,000
Mental health counseling: $25,000
Disability/Loss of earnings: $25,000
Rehabilitation: N/A
Funeral: $1,000
Attorney fees: $1,000, up to 15% of total award
Replacement services: N/A
Pain and suffering: No
Property loss: No

Fine print: Contributory conduct can reduce your claim

Note: These laws change frequently. Check with the prosecutor for any changes which affect your case.

Louisiana

Persons eligible: injured party, spouse, children, parents

Compensable crimes:

Assault and battery	Motor vehicle crime
Child physical abuse	Rape
Child sexual abuse	Robbery
Domestic abuse	Sex offenses
Homicide	Spouse abuse

Maximum Award: $10,000

Emergency Funds: $500

Time limit for reporting crime: N/A

Time limit for filing application: 1 year

Processing time for filing application: 45 weeks

Processing time for emergency funds: 6 days

Time limit for first appeal: 5 days

Method of payment: installments

Compensable losses
    Medical: $1,000
    Mental health counseling: $2,500
    Disability/Loss of earnings: $1,000
    Rehabilitation: $1,000
    Funeral: $1,000
    Attorney fees: $1,000, up to 50 hours on top of max. award
    Replacement services: $1,000
    Pain and suffering: No
    Property loss: $5,000

Fine print: Contributory conduct can reduce your claim

Note: These laws change frequently. Check with the prosecutor for any changes which affect your case.

Maine

Persons eligible: injured party

Compensable crimes:

Assault and battery

Child physical abuse

Child sexual abuse

Domestic abuse

Drunk driving

Homicide

Motor vehicle crime

Robbery

Sex offenses

Maximum Award: $5,000

Emergency Funds: No

Time limit for reporting crime: 5 days

Time limit for filing application: 1 year

Processing time for filing application: 30 - 60 days

Processing time for emergency funds: N/A

Time limit for first appeal: 30 days

Method of payment: lump sum/ installment

Compensable losses

Medical: Yes

Mental health counseling: Yes

Disability/Loss of earnings: Yes

Rehabilitation: Yes

Funeral: Yes

Attorney fees: No

Replacement services: Yes

Pain and suffering: No

Property loss: No

Fine print: Contributory conduct can reduce your claim

Note: These laws change frequently. Check with the prosecutor for any changes which affect your case.

Maryland

Persons eligible: injured party, spouse, children, parents, siblings

Compensable crimes:

Assault and battery

Child physical abuse

Child sexual abuse

Domestic abuse

Homicide

Motor vehicle crime

Rape

Sex offenses

Spouse abuse

Maximum Award: $45,000

Emergency Funds: $1,000

Time limit for reporting crime: 2 days

Time limit for filing application: 1 year

Processing time for filing application: 10 weeks

Processing time for emergency funds: 10 days

Time limit for first appeal: 30 days

Method of payment: lump sum/installments/direct to vendors

Compensable losses

Medical: $45,000

Mental health counseling: $45,000

Disability/Loss of earnings: $45,000

Rehabilitation: $45,000

Funeral: $1,000

Attorney fees: $1,000; $50 prep; $65 before the board

Replacement services: $1,000

Pain and suffering: No

Property loss: No

Fine print: Contributory conduct can reduce your claim

Note: These laws change frequently. Check with the prosecutor for any changes which affect your case.

Massachusetts

Persons eligible: injured party, spouse, children, parents, siblings

Compensable crimes:

Assault and battery
Child physical abuse
Child sexual abuse
Domestic abuse
Drunk driving
Homicide

Motor vehicle crime
Rape
Robbery
Sex offenses
Spouse abuse

Maximum Award: $25,000

Emergency Funds: 0

Time limit for reporting crime: 2 days

Time limit for filing application: 1 year

Processing time for filing application: 32 weeks

Processing time for emergency funds: N/A

Time limit for first appeal: 15 days

Method of payment: lump sum and/or to vendors

Compensable losses
Medical: $1,000
Mental health counseling: $1,000
Disability/Loss of earnings: $1,000
Rehabilitation: $1,000
Funeral: $1,000
Attorney fees: $1,000; up to 15% of the total award
Replacement services: $1,000
Pain and suffering: No
Property loss: No

Fine print: Contributory conduct can reduce your claim

Note: These laws change frequently. Check with the prosecutor for any changes which affect your case.

121

Michigan

Persons eligible: injured party, spouse, children, parents, siblings

Compensable crimes:

Assault and battery	Motor vehicle crime
Child physical abuse	Rape
Child sexual abuse	Robbery
Domestic abuse	Sex offenses
Drunk driving	Spouse abuse
Homicide	

Maximum Award: $15,000

Emergency Funds: $500

Time limit for reporting crime: 2 days

Time limit for filing application: 1 year

Processing time for filing application: 22 weeks

Processing time for emergency funds: 30 days

Time limit for first appeal: 30 days

Method of payment: lump sum/installments/direct to vendors

Compensable losses
> **Medical:** $1,000
> **Mental health counseling:** $1,000
> **Disability/Loss of earnings:** $1,000
> **Rehabilitation:** $1,000
> **Funeral:** $1,000
> **Attorney fees:** No
> **Replacement services:** $1,000
> **Pain and suffering:** No
> **Property loss:** $1,000

Fine print: Contributory conduct can reduce your claim

Note: These laws change frequently. Check with the prosecutor for any changes which affect your case.

Minnesota

Persons eligible: injured party, spouse, children, parents, siblings

Compensable crimes:

Assault and battery	Homicide
Child physical abuse	Rape
Child sexual abuse	Robbery
Domestic abuse	Sex offenses
Drunk driving	Spouse abuse

Maximum Award: $50,000

Emergency Funds: $5000

Time limit for reporting crime: 5 days

Time limit for filing application: 1 year

Processing time for filing application: 14 weeks

Processing time for emergency funds: 12 days

Time limit for first appeal: 30 days

Method of payment: lump sum/ installments

Compensable losses
    Medical: $1,000
    Mental health counseling: $1,000
    Disability/Loss of earnings: $1,000
    Rehabilitation: $1,000
    Funeral: $1,000
    Attorney fees: $1,000
    Replacement services: $1,000
    Pain and suffering: No
    Property loss: No

Fine print: Contributory conduct can reduce your claim

Note: These laws change frequently. Check with the prosecutor for any changes which affect your case.

Mississippi

Persons eligible: injured party, spouse, children,

Compensable crimes:

Assault and battery	Motor vehicle crime
Child physical abuse	Rape
Child sexual abuse	Robbery
Domestic abuse	Sex offenses
Drunk driving	Spouse abuse
Homicide	

Maximum Award: $10,000

Emergency Funds: N/A

Time limit for reporting crime: 3 days

Time limit for filing application: 1 year

Processing time for filing application: N/A

Processing time for emergency funds: N/A

Time limit for first appeal: N/A

Method of payment: lump sum and/or to vendors

Compensable losses
    Medical: $10,000
    Mental health counseling: $1,000
    Disability/Loss of earnings: $150/week for 20 weeks
    Rehabilitation: $10,000
    Funeral: $1,000
    Attorney fees: N/A
    Replacement services: N/A
    Pain and suffering: No
    Property loss: No

Fine print: Contributory conduct can reduce your claim

Note: These laws change frequently. Check with the prosecutor for any changes which affect your case.

Missouri

Persons eligible: injured party, spouse, children, parents, siblings

Compensable crimes:

Assault and battery	Homicide
Child physical abuse	Motor vehicle crime
Child sexual abuse	Rape
Domestic abuse	Sex offenses
Drunk driving	Spouse abuse

Maximum Award: $10,000

Emergency Funds: $100

Time limit for reporting crime: 2 days

Time limit for filing application: 1 year

Processing time for filing application: 30 weeks

Processing time for emergency funds: 30 days

Time limit for first appeal: 30 days

Method of payment: lump sum

Compensable losses
> **Medical:** $1,000
> **Mental health counseling:** $1,000
> **Disability/Loss of earnings:** $1,000
> **Rehabilitation:** N/A
> **Funeral:** $1,000
> **Attorney fees:** $1,000; up to 15% of total award
> **Replacement services:** N/A
> **Pain and suffering:** No
> **Property loss:** No

Fine print: Contributory conduct can reduce your claim

Note: These laws change frequently. Check with the prosecutor for any changes which affect your case.

Montana

Persons eligible: injured party, spouse, children, parents, siblings

Compensable crimes:

Assault and battery	Rape
Child physical abuse	Robbery
Child sexual abuse	Sex offenses
Domestic abuse	Spouse abuse
Homicide	

Maximum Award: $25,000

Emergency Funds: 0

Time limit for reporting crime: 3 days

Time limit for filing application: 1 year

Processing time for filing application: 7 weeks

Processing time for emergency funds: 7 days

Time limit for first appeal: 30 days

Method of payment: lump sum/installments/direct to vendors

Compensable losses
Medical: $25,000
Mental health counseling: $25,000
Disability/Loss of earnings: $25,000
Rehabilitation: $25,000
Funeral: $1,000
Attorney fees: $1,000
Replacement services: N/A
Pain and suffering: No
Property loss: No

Fine print: Contributory conduct can reduce your claim

Note: These laws change frequently. Check with the prosecutor for any changes which affect your case.

Nebraska

Persons eligible: injured party, spouse, children, parents, siblings

Compensable crimes:

Assault and battery
Child physical abuse
Child sexual abuse
Domestic abuse
Drunk driving

Homicide
Rape
Sex offenses
Spouse abuse

Maximum Award: $10,000

Emergency Funds: $500

Time limit for reporting crime: 3 days

Time limit for filing application: 2 years

Processing time for filing application: 6 weeks

Processing time for emergency funds: N/A

Time limit for first appeal: 30 days

Method of payment: lump sum/installments

Compensable losses
Medical: $1,000
Mental health counseling: $2,000
Disability/Loss of earnings: $1,000
Rehabilitation: $5,000
Funeral: $1,000
Attorney fees: $500
Replacement services: $1,000
Pain and suffering: No
Property loss: No

Fine print: Contributory conduct can reduce your claim

Note: These laws change frequently. Check with the prosecutor for any
changes which affect your case.

Nevada

Persons eligible: injured party, spouse, children, parents

Compensable crimes:

Assault and battery	Homicide
Child physical abuse	Rape
Child sexual abuse	Robbery
Domestic abuse	Sex offenses
Drunk driving	Spouse abuse

Maximum Award: $15,000

Emergency Funds: $500

Time limit for reporting crime: 5 days

Time limit for filing application: 1 year

Processing time for filing application: 12 weeks

Processing time for emergency funds: 20 days

Time limit for first appeal: 15 days

Method of payment: lump sum/installment/direct to vendors

Compensable losses
   Medical: $1,000
   Mental health counseling: $1,000
   Disability/Loss of earnings: up to $200/week
   Rehabilitation: $1,000
   Funeral: up to $1,000
   Attorney fees: $1,000
   Replacement services: $1,000
   Pain and suffering: No
   Property loss: $1,000

Fine print: Contributory conduct can reduce your claim

Note: These laws change frequently. Check with the prosecutor for any changes which affect your case.

New Hampshire

Persons eligible: injured party, spouse, children, parents

Compensable crimes:

Assault and battery	Motor vehicle crime
Child physical abuse	Rape
Child sexual abuse	Robbery
Domestic abuse	Sex offenses
Drunk driving	Spouse abuse
Homicide	

Maximum Award: $5,000

Emergency Funds: No

Time limit for reporting crime: 5 days

Time limit for filing application: 1 year

Processing time for filing application: 14 weeks

Processing time for emergency funds: N/A

Time limit for first appeal: 14 days

Method of payment: lump sum/ installment

Compensable losses
    Medical: $5,000
    Mental health counseling: $2,000
    Disability/Loss of earnings: $5,000
    Rehabilitation: Yes
    Funeral: $2,000
    Attorney fees: No
    Replacement services: Yes
    Pain and suffering: No
    Property loss: No

Fine print: Contributory conduct can reduce your claim

Note: These laws change frequently. Check with the prosecutor for any changes which affect your case.

New Jersey

Persons eligible: injured party, spouse, children, parents, siblings

Compensable crimes:

Assault and battery	Rape
Child physical abuse	Robbery
Child sexual abuse	Sex offenses
Domestic abuse	Spouse abuse
Homicide	

Maximum Award: $25,000

Emergency Funds: $1,500

Time limit for reporting crime: 90 days

Time limit for filing application: 2 years

Processing time for filing application: 26 weeks

Processing time for emergency funds: 5 days

Time limit for first appeal: 20 days

Method of payment: lump sum/installment/direct to vendors

Compensable losses
> **Medical:** $1,000
> **Mental health counseling:** $1,000
> **Disability/Loss of earnings:** $1,000
> **Rehabilitation:** $1,000
> **Funeral:** $1,000
> **Attorney fees:** $1,000
> **Replacement services:** $1,000
> **Pain and suffering:** No
> **Property loss:** $1,000

Fine print: Contributory conduct can reduce your claim

Note: These laws change frequently. Check with the prosecutor for any changes which affect your case.

New Mexico

Persons eligible: injured party, spouse, children, parents, siblings

Compensable crimes:

Assault and battery	Homicide
Child sexual abuse	Motor vehicle crime
Drunk driving	Rape

Maximum Award: $12,500

Emergency Funds: $1,500

Time limit for reporting crime: 30 days

Time limit for filing application: 1 year

Processing time for filing application: N/A

Processing time for emergency funds: N/A

Time limit for first appeal: N/A

Method of payment: lump sum/installments

Compensable losses
>**Medical:** $10,000
>**Mental health counseling:** $10,000
>**Disability/Loss of earnings:** $5,200
>**Rehabilitation:** $10,000
>**Funeral:** No
>**Attorney fees:** No
>**Replacement services:** $10,000
>**Pain and suffering:** No
>**Property loss:** No

Fine print: Contributory conduct can reduce your claim

Note: These laws change frequently. Check with the prosecutor for any changes which affect your case.

New York

Persons eligible: injured party, spouse, children, parents, siblings

Compensable crimes:

Assault and battery	Motor vehicle crime
Child physical abuse	Rape
Child sexual abuse	Robbery
Domestic abuse	Sex offenses
Drunk driving	Spouse abuse
Homicide	

Maximum Award: unlimited

Emergency Funds: 0

Time limit for reporting crime: 7 days

Time limit for filing application: 1 year

Processing time for filing application: 16 weeks

Processing time for emergency funds: 7 days

Time limit for first appeal: 30 days

Method of payment: lump sum/installment

Compensable losses
    Medical: $1,000
    Mental health counseling: $1,000
    Disability/Loss of earnings: $30,000
    Rehabilitation: $1,000
    Funeral: $1,000
    Attorney fees: $1,000
    Replacement services: $1,000
    Pain and suffering: No
    Property loss: $500

Fine print: Contributory conduct can reduce your claim

Note: These laws change frequently. Check with the prosecutor for any changes which affect your case.

North Carolina

Persons eligible: injured party, spouse, children, parents, siblings

Compensable crimes:

Assault and battery	Motor vehicle crime
Child physical abuse	Rape
Child sexual abuse	Robbery
Domestic abuse	Sex offenses
Homicide	Spouse abuse

Maximum Award: $22,000

Emergency Funds: $5000

Time limit for reporting crime: 3 days

Time limit for filing application: 1 year

Processing time for filing application: 13 weeks

Processing time for emergency funds: 3 days

Time limit for first appeal: 60 days

Method of payment: lump sum/installment

Compensable losses
> **Medical:** $20,000
> **Mental health counseling:** $20,000
> **Disability/Loss of earnings:** $4,800
> **Rehabilitation:** $1,000
> **Funeral:** $1,000
> **Attorney fees:** No
> **Replacement services:** $4,800
> **Pain and suffering:** No
> **Property loss:** No

Fine print: Contributory conduct can reduce your claim

Note: These laws change frequently. Check with the prosecutor for any changes which affect your case.

North Dakota

Persons eligible: injured party

Compensable crimes:

Assault and battery	Homicide
Child physical abuse	Rape
Child sexual abuse	Robbery
Domestic abuse	Sex offenses
Drunk driving	Spouse abuse

Maximum Award: $25,000

Emergency Funds: 0

Time limit for reporting crime: 3 days

Time limit for filing application: 1 year

Processing time for filing application: 10 weeks

Processing time for emergency funds: N/A

Time limit for first appeal: 30 days

Method of payment: lump sum/installments

Compensable losses
    Medical: $1,000
    Mental health counseling: $1,000
    Disability/Loss of earnings: $1,000
    Rehabilitation: $1,000
    Funeral: $1,000
    Attorney fees: $1,000
    Replacement services: $1,000
    Pain and suffering: No
    Property loss: No

Fine print: Contributory conduct can reduce your claim

Note: These laws change frequently. Check with the prosecutor for any changes which affect your case.

Ohio

Persons eligible: Injured party, good Samaritan, dependent of deceased victim, someone who has paid the expenses of a victim

Compensable crimes:

Assault and battery	Motor vehicle crime
Child physical abuse	Rape
Child sexual abuse	Robbery
Domestic abuse	Sex offenses
Homicide	Spouse abuse

Maximum Award: $50,000

Emergency Funds: 0

Time limit for reporting crime: 72 hours

Time limit for filing application: 2 years

Processing time for filing application: 1 yr. (non-death), 2 yrs. (death)

Processing time for emergency funds: N/A

Time limit for first appeal: 21 days

Method of payment: lump sum

Compensable losses
Medical: Yes
Mental health counseling: Yes
Disability/Loss of earnings: Yes
Rehabilitation: Yes
Funeral: $2,500
Attorney fees: No, however the agency will provide attorneys to assist applicants with their claims.
Replacement services: Yes
Pain and suffering: No
Property loss: No

Fine print: Contributory conduct can reduce your claim

Note: These laws change frequently. Check with the prosecutor for any changes which affect your case.

Oklahoma

Persons eligible: injured party, spouse, children, parents, siblings

Compensable crimes:

Assault and battery	Motor vehicle crime
Child physical abuse	Rape
Child sexual abuse	Robbery
Domestic abuse	Sex offenses
Homicide	Spouse abuse

Maximum Award: $10,000

Emergency Funds: $500

Time limit for reporting crime: 3 days

Time limit for filing application: 1 year

Processing time for filing application: 15 weeks

Processing time for emergency funds: 12 days

Time limit for first appeal: 30 days

Method of payment: lump sum/installments

Compensable losses
   Medical: $10,000
   Mental health counseling: $10,000
   Disability/Loss of earnings: $10,000
   Rehabilitation: $10,000
   Funeral: $1,000
   Attorney fees: $500
   Replacement services: $10,000
   Pain and suffering: No
   Property loss: No

Fine print: Contributory conduct can reduce your claim

Note: These laws change frequently. Check with the prosecutor for any changes which affect your case.

Oregon

Persons eligible: injured party, spouse, children, parents, siblings

Compensable crimes:

Assault and battery	Motor vehicle crime
Child physical abuse	Rape
Child sexual abuse	Robbery
Domestic abuse	Sex offenses
Drunk driving	Spouse abuse
Homicide	

Maximum Award: $23,000

Emergency Funds: 0

Time limit for reporting crime: 3 days

Time limit for filing application: 1 year

Processing time for filing application: 18 weeks

Processing time for emergency funds: 7 days

Time limit for first appeal: 60 days

Method of payment: lump sum/installments

Compensable losses
  Medical: $10,000
  Mental health counseling: $10,000
  Disability/Loss of earnings: $10,000
  Rehabilitation: $3,000
  Funeral: $1,000
  Attorney fees: $500
  Replacement services: N/A
  Pain and suffering: No
  Property loss: No

Fine print: Contributory conduct can reduce your claim

Note: These laws change frequently. Check with the prosecutor for any changes which affect your case.

Pennsylvania

Persons eligible: injured party, spouse, children, parents, siblings

Compensable crimes:

Assault and battery	Rape
Child physical abuse	Robbery
Child sexual abuse	Sex offenses
Domestic abuse	Spouse abuse
Homicide	

Maximum Award: $35,000

Emergency Funds: $1,000

Time limit for reporting crime: 72 days

Time limit for filing application: 1 year

Processing time for filing application: 20 weeks

Processing time for emergency funds: 28 days

Time limit for first appeal: 20 days

Method of payment: lump sum/installment

Compensable losses
>   **Medical:** $35,000
>   **Mental health counseling:** $35,000
>   **Disability/Loss of earnings:** $10,000
>   **Rehabilitation:** $35,000
>   **Funeral:** $1,000
>   **Attorney fees:** $1,000;15% of total award or $75,
>   whichever is less
>   **Replacement services:** $35,000
>   **Pain and suffering:** No
>   **Property loss:** No

Fine print: Contributory conduct can reduce your claim

Note: These laws change frequently. Check with the prosecutor for any changes which affect your case.

Rhode Island

Persons eligible: injured party, spouse, children, parents, siblings

Compensable crimes:

Assault and battery	Motor vehicle crime
Child physical abuse	Rape
Child sexual abuse	Robbery
Domestic abuse	Sex offenses
Drunk driving	Spouse abuse
Homicide	

Maximum Award: $25,000

Emergency Funds: 0

Time limit for reporting crime: 10 days

Time limit for filing application: 3 years

Processing time for filing application: 104 weeks

Processing time for emergency funds: N/A

Time limit for first appeal: 20 days

Method of payment: lump sum

Compensable losses
Medical: $1,000
Mental health counseling: $1,000
Disability/Loss of earnings: $1,000
Rehabilitation: $1,000
Funeral: $1,000
Attorney fees: $2,000
Replacement services: $1,000
Pain and suffering: $1,000
Property loss: No

Fine print: Contributory conduct can reduce your claim

Note: These laws change frequently. Check with the prosecutor for any changes which affect your case.

South Carolina

Persons eligible: injured party, spouse, children, parents, siblings

Compensable crimes:

Assault and battery	Homicide
Child physical abuse	Motor vehicle crime
Child sexual abuse	Rape
Domestic abuse	Sex offenses
Drunk driving	

Maximum Award: $10,000

Emergency Funds: $1,500

Time limit for reporting crime: 2 days

Time limit for filing application: 1 year

Processing time for filing application: 9 weeks

Processing time for emergency funds: 2 days

Time limit for first appeal: 30 days

Method of payment: lump sum/installments

Compensable losses
> **Medical:** $1,000
> **Mental health counseling: $1,000**
> **Disability/Loss of earnings:** $1,000
> **Rehabilitation:** $1,000
> **Funeral:** $1,000
> **Attorney fees:** $1,000; 10% of the award
> **Replacement services:** $1,000
> **Pain and suffering:** No
> **Property loss:** No

Fine print:

Note: These laws change frequently. Check with the prosecutor for any changes which affect your case.

South Dakota

Persons eligible: injured party, spouse, children, parents, good Samaritan

Compensable crimes:

Assault and battery	Motor vehicle crime
Child physical abuse	Rape
Child sexual abuse	Robbery
Domestic abuse	Sex offenses
Drunk driving	Spouse abuse
Homicide	

Maximum Award: $10,000

Emergency Funds: $1,000

Time limit for reporting crime: 5 days

Time limit for filing application: 1 year

Processing time for filing application: 3 months

Processing time for emergency funds: 10 days

Time limit for first appeal: 15 days

Method of payment: direct to vendors

Compensable losses
  Medical: Yes
  Mental health counseling: Yes
  Disability/Loss of earnings: N/A
  Rehabilitation: Yes
  Funeral: $4,500
  Attorney fees: No
  Replacement services: Yes
  Pain and suffering: No
  Property loss: No

Fine print: Contributory conduct can reduce your claim

Note: These laws change frequently. Check with the prosecutor for any changes which affect your case.

Tennessee

Persons eligible: injured party, spouse, children, parents, siblings

Compensable crimes:

Assault and battery

Child physical abuse

Child sexual abuse

Drunk driving

Homicide

Rape

Robbery

Sex offenses

Spouse abuse

Maximum Award: $5,000

Emergency Funds: $500

Time limit for reporting crime: 2 days

Time limit for filing application: 1 year

Processing time for filing application: 12 weeks

Processing time for emergency funds: 15 days

Time limit for first appeal: 30 days

Method of payment: lump sum

Compensable losses

Medical: $1,000

Mental health counseling: $1,000

Disability/Loss of earnings: $1,000

Rehabilitation: N/A

Funeral: $1,000

Attorney fees: $1,000; up to 15% of total award

Replacement services: N/A

Pain and suffering: $2,500

Property loss: No

Fine print: Contributory conduct can reduce your claim

Note: These laws change frequently. Check with the prosecutor for any changes which affect your case.

142

Texas

Persons eligible: injured party, spouse, children, parents, siblings

Compensable crimes:

Assault and battery

Child physical abuse

Child sexual abuse

Domestic abuse

Drunk driving

Homicide

Motor vehicle crime

Rape

Robbery

Sex offenses

Spouse abuse

Maximum Award: $25,000

Emergency Funds: $1,500

Time limit for reporting crime: 3 days

Time limit for filing application: 1 year

Processing time for filing application: 22 weeks

Processing time for emergency funds: 3 days

Time limit for first appeal: 20 days

Method of payment: lump sum/installments

Compensable losses

Medical: $1,000

Mental health counseling: $1,000

Disability/Loss of earnings: $1,000

Rehabilitation: $1,000

Funeral: $1,000

Attorney fees: $1,000

Replacement services: $1,000

Pain and suffering: No

Property loss: No

Fine print: Contributory conduct can reduce your claim

Note: These laws change frequently. Check with the prosecutor for any changes which affect your case.

Utah

Persons eligible: injured party, spouse, children, parents, siblings

Compensable crimes:

Assault and battery	Motor vehicle crime
Child physical abuse	Rape
Child sexual abuse	Robbery
Domestic abuse	Sex offenses
Drunk driving	Spouse abuse
Homicide	

Maximum Award: $50,000

Emergency Funds: $1,000

Time limit for reporting crime: 7 days

Time limit for filing application: 1 year

Processing time for filing application: 4 weeks

Processing time for emergency funds: 4 days

Time limit for first appeal: 20 days

Method of payment: lump sum/installments

Compensable losses
    Medical: $1,000
    Mental health counseling: $5,000
    Disability/Loss of earnings: $1,000
    Rehabilitation: $1,000
    Funeral: $1,000
    Attorney fees: No
    Replacement services: $1,000
    Pain and suffering: No
    Property loss: No

Fine print: Contributory conduct can reduce your claim

Note: These laws change frequently. Check with the prosecutor for any changes which affect your case.

Vermont

Persons eligible: injured party, dependent

Compensable crimes:

Assault and battery	Drunk driving
Child sexual abuse	Homicide
Domestic abuse	Sex offenses

Maximum Award: $10,000

Emergency Funds: $250

Time limit for reporting crime: No

Time limit for filing application: No

Processing time for filing application: 3 months, approx.

Processing time for emergency funds: 3 to 4 days

Time limit for first appeal: 30 days

Method of payment: direct to vendors

Compensable losses
> **Medical:** $10,000
> **Mental health counseling:** $3,000
> **Disability/Loss of earnings:** $1,500 per month
> **Rehabilitation:** Yes
> **Funeral:** $4,500
> **Attorney fees:** No
> **Replacement services:** Yes
> **Pain and suffering:** No
> **Property loss:** No

Fine print: Contributory conduct can reduce your claim

Note: These laws change frequently. Check with the prosecutor for any changes which affect your case.

Virgin Islands

Persons eligible: injured party, spouse, children, parents, siblings

Compensable crimes:

Assault and battery	Robbery
Child sexual abuse	Sex offenses
Homicide	Spouse abuse
Rape	

Maximum Award: $25,000

Emergency Funds: 0

Time limit for reporting crime: 7 days

Time limit for filing application: 2 years

Processing time for filing application: 27 weeks

Processing time for emergency funds: N/A

Time limit for first appeal: N/A

Method of payment: installments

Compensable losses
> **Medical:** $1,000
> **Mental health counseling:** $1,000
> **Disability/Loss of earnings:** $1,000
> **Rehabilitation:** $1,000
> **Funeral:** $1,000
> **Attorney fees:** $1,000
> **Replacement services:** $25,000
> **Pain and suffering:** $1,000
> **Property loss:** No

Fine print: Contributory conduct can reduce your claim

Note: These laws change frequently. Check with the prosecutor for any changes which affect your case.

Virginia

Persons eligible: injured party, spouse, children, parents, siblings

Compensable crimes:

Assault and battery	Homicide
Child physical abuse	Rape
Child sexual abuse	Robbery
Domestic abuse	Sex offenses
Drunk driving	Spouse abuse

Maximum Award: $15,000

Emergency Funds: $2,000

Time limit for reporting crime: 5 days

Time limit for filing application: 1 year

Processing time for filing application: 8 weeks

Processing time for emergency funds: 30 days

Time limit for first appeal: 20 days

Method of payment: lump sum/installment/direct to vendor

Compensable losses
  Medical: $1,000
  Mental health counseling: $1,000
  Disability/Loss of earnings: $1,000
  Rehabilitation: $1,000
  Funeral: $1,000
  Attorney fees: No
  Replacement services: $1,000
  Pain and suffering: No
  Property loss: No

Fine print: Contributory conduct can reduce your claim

Note: These laws change frequently. Check with the prosecutor for any changes which affect your case.

Washington

Persons eligible: injured party, spouse, children, parents, siblings

Compensable crimes:

Assault and battery	Motor vehicle crime
Child physical abuse	Rape
Child sexual abuse	Robbery
Domestic abuse	Sex offenses
Drunk driving	Spouse abuse
Homicide	

Maximum Award: $20,000

Emergency Funds: 0

Time limit for reporting crime: 3 days

Time limit for filing application: 1 year

Processing time for filing application: 4 weeks

Processing time for emergency funds: N/A

Time limit for first appeal: 60 days

Method of payment: lump sum/installments

Compensable losses
Medical: $1,000
Mental health counseling: $1,000
Disability/Loss of earnings: $20,000
Rehabilitation: $5,000
Funeral: $1,000
Attorney fees: No
Replacement services: N/A
Pain and suffering: No
Property loss: $1,000

Fine print: Contributory conduct can reduce your claim

Note: These laws change frequently. Check with the prosecutor for any changes which affect your case.

148

West Virginia

Persons eligible: injured party, spouse, children, parents, siblings

Compensable crimes:

Assault and battery	Motor vehicle crime
Child physical abuse	Rape
Child sexual abuse	Robbery
Domestic abuse	Sex offenses
Drunk driving	Spouse abuse
Homicide	

Maximum Award: $50,000

Emergency Funds: 0

Time limit for reporting crime: 3 days

Time limit for filing application: 2 years

Processing time for filing application: 4 weeks

Processing time for emergency funds: N/A

Time limit for first appeal: 2 days

Method of payment: lump sum

Compensable losses
    Medical: $35,000
    Mental health counseling: $1,000
    Disability/Loss of earnings: $1,000
    Rehabilitation: $1,000
    Funeral: $1,000
    Attorney fees: $1,000
    Replacement services: $1,000
    Pain and suffering: $15,000
    Property loss: No

Fine print: Contributory conduct can reduce your claim

Note: These laws change frequently. Check with the prosecutor for any changes which affect your case.

Wisconsin

Persons eligible: injured party, spouse, children, parents, siblings

Compensable crimes:

Assault and battery	Motor vehicle crime
Child physical abuse	Rape
Child sexual abuse	Robbery
Domestic abuse	Sex offenses
Drunk driving	Spouse abuse
Homicide	

Maximum Award: $40,000

Emergency Funds: $500

Time limit for reporting crime: 5 days

Time limit for filing application: 1 year

Processing time for filing application: 14 weeks

Processing time for emergency funds: N/A

Time limit for first appeal: 30 days

Method of payment: lump sum/installment/direct to vendor

Compensable losses
>   **Medical:** $1,000
>   **Mental health counseling:** $1,000
>   **Disability/Loss of earnings:** N/A
>   **Rehabilitation:** $1,000
>   **Funeral:** $1,000
>   **Attorney fees:** $1,000; up to 10% of the award
>   **Replacement services:** $1,000
>   **Pain and suffering:** No
>   **Property loss:** $200

Fine print: Contributory conduct can reduce your claim

Note: These laws change frequently. Check with the prosecutor for any changes which affect your case.

Wyoming

Persons eligible: injured party, spouse, children, parents, siblings

Compensable crimes:

Assault and battery	Homicide
Child physical abuse	Rape
Child sexual abuse	Robbery
Domestic abuse	Sex offenses
Drunk driving	Spouse abuse

Maximum Award: $10,000

Emergency Funds: $1,000

Time limit for reporting crime: N/A

Time limit for filing application: 1 year

Processing time for filing application: 5 weeks

Processing time for emergency funds: 5 days

Time limit for first appeal: N/A

Method of payment: lump sum and/or to vendors

Compensable losses
Medical: $1,000
Mental health counseling: $1,000
Disability/Loss of earnings: $500
Rehabilitation: $1,000
Funeral: $1,000
Attorney fees: No
Replacement services: $500
Pain and suffering: No
Property loss: No

Fine print: Contributory conduct can reduce your claim

Note: These laws change frequently. Check with the prosecutor for any changes which affect your case.

Appendix D
Sample Filled-in Form

The following is a photo-copy of the application form you must complete in order to obtain compensation in the state of California. California has the longest application form of any state, so it should be of help to someone in any other state.

The forms we obtained from the various states came in many different forms, sizes, shapes and formats. Since the states require you to use their actual application forms, you cannot simply remove and submit the form you find in this book. However, in Appendix B of this book you will find a complete list of state officials who will send you the actual application forms you require.

You will be ready to correctly complete the official application form, when it arrives, by reviewing the form which follows.

Application For Crime Victim Compensation

State of California
Board of Control
Victims of Crime Program

Please read the instructions in the accompanying booklet before completing the application. PRINT IN BLACK INK OR TYPE.

Section 1A
Applicant Information

Applicant's Name (First, Middle, Last)
Ben T. Hellenbeck

Street Address: 124 W. 14th St.   City: Palo Verde   State: CA   Zip: 90641

Home Phone: (714) 555-1212   Work Phone: (714) 555-4300

Date of Birth (Mo. Day Yr.): 4/21/49   Social Security Number: 296-17-4444   Sex: ☒Male ☐Female

Relationship to Victim: Victim

Are you filling this claim on behalf of a child under 18? ☒ No ☐ Yes - If yes, complete the following subsection:

CHILD'S NAME AND RELATIONSHIP TO VICTIM AND APPLICANT

Child's Name (First, Middle, Last)

Date of Birth (Mo. Day Yr.)   Social Security Number   Sex: ☐Male ☐Female

Relationship to Victim (in Section 1B)   Relationship to Applicant

Section 1B
Victim Information

The victim is the person whose name appears on the crime report as the victim

Victim's Name (First, Middle, Last) Same as Applicant

Street Address   City   State   Zip

Home Phone ( )   Work Phone ( )

Date of Birth (Mo. Day Yr.)   Social Security Number   Sex: ☐Male ☐Female

Is the victim a dependent/ward of the court? ☐ Yes ☒ No

154

Is the victim deceased? ☐ Yes ☒ No   If the victim is deceased, are you claiming Funeral/Burial loss? ☐ Yes ☐ No
If Yes, date of death:

Section 1C
Felony Conviction Information

Have you been convicted of a felony committed after December 31, 1988? ☐ Yes ☒ No
(You may indicate 'no' if the conviction was dismissed pursuant to Penal Code Section 1203.4 or for which you have received a certificate of rehabilitation pursuant to Penal Code Section 4852.01.)

Are you presently on probation, serving time in a correctional institution or on parole as a result of this felony conviction? ☐ Yes ☒ No

Section 2
Related Claims

Have you (or will you) any other applications been filed due to this crime? ☐ Yes ☒ No   (If Yes, complete below)
Have you filed applications for other crimes? ☐ Yes ☒ No   (If Yes, complete below)

If more space is needed, continue in Section 10

Name of Applicant

Claim No.   Filed for Loss of Support?
                        ☐ Yes ☐ No

Date of Birth (Mo. Day Yr.)   Social Security Number

Name of Applicant

Claim No.   Filed for Loss of Support?
                        ☐ Yes ☐ No

Date of Birth (Mo. Day Yr.)   Social Security Number

Name of Applicant

Claim No.   Filed for Loss of Support?
                        ☐ Yes ☐ No

Date of Birth (Mo. Day Yr.)   Social Security Number

Section 3
Law Enforcement/Crime Information

Name of Law Enforcement Agency Notified   ☒ Police ☐ Sheriff ☐ Highway Patrol
Santa Rosita P.D.   ☐ Other (describe):

Address of Law Enforcement Agency   City *Santa Rosita*   State *CA*   Zip *94612*
141 S. Central Ave.

Date of Report (Mo. Day Yr.)   Date of Crime (Mo. Day Yr.)   Name of Suspect (if known):
4/22/94   *4/22/94*   *Jack Len Hyde*

Crime Report Number   Crime Code   Briefly Describe Crime (Assault, Robbery, etc.)
94-07694   *451*   *Assault*

Location of Crime: Street   County   City   State   Zip
Main Street   *Los Angeles* *Santa Rosita*   *CA*   *94612*

Your claim will be processed sooner if a crime report is attached to your application

Page 5   Continued on next page

Application For Crime Victim Compensation (continued)

Section 4

Medical/Mental Health Counseling/ Dental/Funeral and Burial Expenses

Attach all bills, receipts, vouchers, etc. If additional space is needed, use extra paper

Provider(s) of Service	Service Dates From	To	Total Amount Billed
Name Santa Rosita Hospital	4/22/94	4/24/94	$ 6,285.94
Address 2940 Ocean Hwy.	Professional License # or Federal I.D. #		
City Santa Rosita State CA Zip 94612			
Phone Number (714) 555-2000			
Will there be additional bills from this Provider? ☒ Yes ☐ No			
Name Jacques Terrapee, Psychiatrist	4/30/94	5/30/94	$ 875.00
Address 2952 Ocean Hwy.	Professional License # or Federal I.D. #		
City Santa Rosita State CA Zip 94612			
Phone Number (714) 555-1342			
Will there be additional bills from this Provider? ☐ Yes ☒ No			
Name			$
Address	Professional License # or Federal I.D. #		
City State Zip			
Phone Number ( )			
Will there be additional bills from this Provider? ☐ Yes ☐ No			

As a result of the crime, were medical items damaged, lost or required? (Glasses, wheelchair, etc.) ☐ Yes ☒ No If yes, describe:
List the provider in the space above and include a copy of the bill.

Section 5

Medical/Mental Health Counselling/ Dental/Funeral and Burial Reimbursement Sources

Medi-Cal	☐ Yes	☒ No	☐ Pending	Renters Insurance	☐ Yes ☒ No ☐ Pending
Medicare A/B	☐ Yes	☒ No	☐ Pending	Liability Insurance	☐ Yes ☒ No ☐ Pending
MIA, CMSP	☐ Yes	☒ No	☐ Pending	Social Security	☐ Yes ☒ No ☐ Pending
Medical/Health Insurance	☐ Yes	☐ No	☒ Pending	Funeral and/or Burial Policy	☐ Yes ☒ No ☐ Pending
Workers Compensation	☐ Yes	☒ No	☐ Pending	Life Insurance	☐ Yes ☒ No ☐ Pending
Auto Insurance	☐ Yes	☒ No	☐ Pending	Veterans Benefits	☐ Yes ☒ No ☐ Pending
Estate Insurance	☐ Yes	☒ No	☐ Pending	Other? Please describe:	
Homeowners Insurance	☐ Yes	☒ No	☐ Pending		

Section 5A

Medi-Cal Number _____   Medicare Number _____

Complete For Any 'Yes' or 'Pending' Answer(s) In Section 5

Attach any explanation of benefits received to date

Insurance Company Wilthay - Pey Insur. Co.   Phone Number (401) 555-0011   Policy/Group No. 0976-24640-A

Address 2500 Simpson Dr.   City Atlanta   State GA   Zip 30624

Policyholder's Name Ben T. Hellenbeck   Policyholder's SSN 296-17-4444   Policyholder's Employer Simi-Conductor Corp.

Section 6

Employment Information

Must be completed even if no income or support loss is claimed

APPLICANT'S Employer Simi-Conductor Corp.   Phone Number (714) 555-5120

Employer's Address 4124 N. Microchip Blvd.   City Palo Verde   State CA   Zip 90641

VICTIM'S Employer Same as Applicant's   Phone Number (   )

Employer's Address _____   City _____   State _____   Zip _____

Self-Employment — If you or the Victim were self-employed at the time of the crime and income loss or support is claimed, provide Federal tax returns, wage statements, schedules and profit and loss statements to verify income for a period of at least one year before the crime.

Continued on next page

Page 6

157

Application For Crime Victim Compensation (continued)

Section 7
Income/Support Loss Information
Attach proof of wages, disability, etc.

Is an income or support loss being claimed? ☐ Yes ☒ No If yes, complete below:

If income loss, give YOUR employer information.

Gross Salary	Hours Worked	
$	☐ Hour ☐ Week	☐ Day ☐ Week
	☐ Day ☐ Month	

Number of persons who rely on victim for support. (Should be the same as on your tax return. Include yourself.)

Is the victim applying for job retraining or employment-oriented rehabilitation?
☐ Yes ☐ No (If yes, a separate form will be mailed to you.)

Person authorizing disability period (Name and Title) — Phone Number ( )

Address — City — State — Zip

Disability Period: From (Mo. Day Yr.) — To (Mo. Day Yr.)

Section 8
Income/Support Loss Reimbursement Sources

Sick Leave	☐ Yes ☒ No ☐ Pending	Auto Insurance	☐ Yes ☒ No ☐ Pending
Workers Compensation	☐ Yes ☒ No ☐ Pending	Mortgage Insurance	☐ Yes ☒ No ☐ Pending
Disability Ins. (Private or State)	☐ Yes ☒ No ☐ Pending	Homeowners/Renters Insurance	☐ Yes ☒ No ☐ Pending
Welfare Benefits	☐ Yes ☒ No ☐ Pending	Life Insurance	☐ Yes ☒ No ☐ Pending
Social Security Disability	☐ Yes ☒ No ☐ Pending	Liability Insurance	☐ Yes ☒ No ☐ Pending
Social Sec. Survivor's Benefits	☐ Yes ☒ No ☐ Pending	Other? Please describe:	

Section 8A
Complete For Any 'Yes' or 'Pending' Answer(s) in Section 8
Attach any explanation of benefits or use additional paper as necessary

Disability Insurance Office Name — Address — City — State — Zip

Welfare Office Name — Address — City — State — Zip

Insurance Company Name — Phone Number ( ) — Policy/Group No.

Address — City — State — Zip

Section 9
Civil Suit
Information

Have you filed suit in connection with the crime?
☐ Yes ☒ No

If no, do you intend to sue?
☐ Yes ☐ No ☒ Undecided

Attorney's Name _None at this time_

Phone Number ( )   State Bar Number

Address _____   City   State   Zip

Section 10
Additional
Information
Or Comments

If additional space is needed please use extra paper

_____

_____

_____

Section 11
Injury Information

If additional space is needed please use extra paper

Briefly Describe Injury

Broken jaw, concussion, internal bleeding, multiple lacerations + bruises, psychological trauma.

Section 12
Applicant's
Representative
Information

Representative's Name _None_

Phone Number ( )

Representative's Address   City   State   Zip

Name of Law Firm or Organization   State Bar Number

☐ VW # _____
☐ Attorney   Are you claiming attorney's fees for representing the victim? ☐ Yes ☐ No
☐ Other, Please explain _____

Continued on next page

159

Application For Crime Victim Compensation (continued)

Section 13

Read each statement, sign and date below.

Print Applicant's Name (if other than victim)

Print Victim's Name

Ben T. Hellanbeck

Authorization To Obtain Information

I hereby voluntarily consent and authorize the State Board of Control or their representatives to review this application and request any employment, funeral, burial or medical records, including diagnosis, prognosis or evaluations, necessary for the verification of the claimed losses. This authorization shall also apply to records of all sources of recovery pertaining to the claimed losses, including but not limited to, governmental or private unemployment and disability insurance, Social Security benefits, Veterans Administration benefits and governmental or private health or medical insurance benefits.

I further authorize the examination of all federal and/or state tax data and/or tax returns for purposes of verifying income and waive all legal privileges pertaining to such, as would otherwise apply.

I understand this authorization is granted for three years pursuant to California Civil Code, Section 1798.24(b). I further authorize the use of a photocopy of this release as being as valid as the original.

Lien Agreement

It is hereby agreed by my signature below that in the event of any recovery by the applicant, by judgment, settlement or otherwise, as a result of any injury to the victim, the State of California shall be entitled to reimbursement in the amount the state may award, to the extent such award is actually recovered, under provisions of Government Code, Section 13959, et seq. The said right of reimbursement shall operate as a lien on any recovery made.

Declaration

I declare under penalty of perjury (Penal Code Sections 72 and 129), that I have read all the questions in this application and, to the best of my information and belief, all my answers are true, correct and complete.

Signature & Date

My signature acknowledges my agreement to each of the statements above and authorizes and assigns payment directly to any medical, funeral or burial provider of service relative to this application should payment of these services be approved by the State Board of Control (unless an objection is declared in Section 10).

The signing of this application does not guarantee payment by the State Board of Control to the applicant or the provider(s) of service.

Applicant's Signature _Ben T. Hollenback_

Date 6/4/94

Submitting Your Application

Remove this application (pages 5-8) at staple and:

Give Completed Application To Your Representative

or

Mail Completed Application To:

State Board of Control
Victims of Crime Program
P.O. Box 3036
Sacramento, CA 95812-3036

Incomplete Applications will not be considered "filed" or accepted until all required information is received.

BC-VOC-100 (Rev. 1/91)

Index

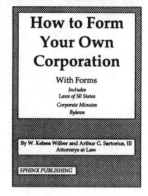

Victims' Rights	12.95
How to File Your Own Divorce	19.95
How to Write Your Own Premarital Agreement	19.95
How to Form Your Own Corporation	19.95
How to Write Your Own Partnership Agreement	19.95
How to Negotiate Real Estate Contracts	14.95
How to Negotiate Real Estate Leases	14.95
The Power of Attorney Handbook	19.95

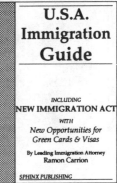

**U.S.A.
Immigration
Guide**

INCLUDING
NEW IMMIGRATION ACT
WITH
*New Opportunities for
Green Cards & Visas*
By Leading Immigration Attorney
Ramon Carrion

SPHINX PUBLISHING

Debtors' Rights	12.95
How to File Your Own Bankruptcy	19.95
U.S.A. Immigration Guide	19.95
Neighbor vs. Neighbor	12.95
How to Register a United States Copyright	14.95
How to Register a United States Trademark	14.95

Florida Legal Guides

Women's Legal Rights in Florida	19.95
How to File for Divorce in Florida	19.95
How to Probate an Estate in Florida	19.95
How to File an Adoption in Florida	19.95
The Florida Power of Attorney Handbook	9.95
How to Start a Business in Florida	16.95
Land Trusts in Florida	19.95
Winning in Florida Small Claims Court	14.95
Real Estate Agents Rights and Duties in Florida	14.95
Landlords' Rights and Duties in Florida	19.95
How to Make a Florida Will	9.95

**Women's
Legal Rights
in Florida**

With Forms
and Caselaw

Includes
Explanation of Laws
Latest Developments
Resource Guide

By Gale Forman Collins
Attorney at Law

SPHINX PUBLISHING

**How to Probate
an Estate
in Florida**

With Forms
Checklists
Statutes

Includes
Formal Administration
Family Administration
Summary Administration

By Gudrun M. Nickel
Attorney at Law

SPHINX PUBLISHING

How to Change Your Name in Florida	14.95
How to Form a Simple Corporation in Florida	19.95
How to Form a Nonprofit Corporation in Florida	14.95
How to File a Guardianship in Florida	19.95
Winning in Florida Traffic Court	14.95
How to Modify Your Florida Divorce Judgment	19.95
How to File a Florida Contruction Lien	19.95

Georgia

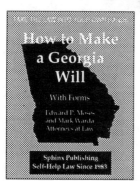

**How to File for Divorce
in Georgia,** $19.95
By Charles T. Robertson II & Edward A. Haman

How to Make a Georgia Will, $9.95
By Edward P. Moses & Mark Warda

**How to Start and Run
a Georgia Business,** $16.95
By Patricia Godwin Dunleavy & Mark Warda

Alabama

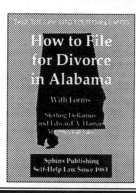

**How to File for Divorce
in Alabama,** $19.95
By Sterling DeRamus & Edward A. Haman

**How to Make an
Alabama Will,** $9.95
By Nancy H. Benjamin & Mark Warda

**How to Start a Business
in Alabama,** $16.95
By Gary G. Stanko & Mark Warda

South Carolina

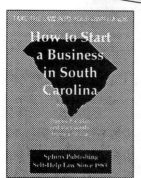

**How to File for Divorce
in South Carolina,** $19.95
By Thomas P. Cullen & Edward A. Haman

**How to Make a South
Carolina Will,** $9.95
By Thomas P. Cullen & Mark Warda

**How to Start a Business
in South Carolina,** $16.95
By Thomas P. Cullen & Mark Warda

Books from other publishers

Patent It Yourself, 3rd Ed.	$36.95
Plan Your Estate With A Living Trust, 2nd Ed.	$19.95
Make Your Own Living Trust	$19.95
How To Win Your Personal Injury Claim	$24.95
Beat the Nursing Home Trap	$18.95
The Living Together Kit, 6th Ed.	$17.95
Simple Contracts for Personal Use, 2nd Ed.	$16.95
Stand Up To The IRS	$19.95
The Independent Paralegal's Handbook, 2nd Ed.	$24.95
How To Write A Business Plan, 4th Ed.	$17.95
Legal Research, How To Find And Understand The Law, 3rd Ed.	$19.95
A Legal Guide For Lesbian And Gay Couples, 6th Ed.	$21.95
Sexual Harrassment On The Job	$14.95

Call us for information about our self-help legal titles for
Alabama, Georgia and South Carolina!

Order Form

To order these publications, please send this form with check or money order to: Sphinx Publishing, P.O. Box 25, Clearwater, FL 34617.

☐ Check Enclosed
☐ Money Order

To order by credit card call:
1-800-226-5291
Or fax this form to (813) 586-5088

We accept VISA, MasterCard, American Express & Discover:

Card number: ☐☐☐☐☐☐☐☐☐☐☐☐☐☐☐☐

Expiration date: ☐☐☐☐

☐ American Express ☐ Visa
☐ MasterCard ☐ Discover

Ship to:

Name_____
Address_____
City_____
State_____ Zip_____

Quantity	Title	Unit Price	Total Price

*Shipping (1 book) $3.50; each add'l $.50
(In Florida, $3.00 for 1-3 books; $.50 ea. add'l.)

Signature

Subtotal	
Sales Tax 7% (FL)	
*Shipping	
Total	